The Complete Englisl

The Complete English Shepherd Guide

Raising Your Puppy and Caring for
Shep--American's Generic Dog

James T. Hammond

2007

Visit www.booksurge.com to order additional copies.

The Complete English Shepherd Guide

Table of Contents

Dedication and Acknowledgement

This book is dedicated to, and an acknowledgement of, all those who so dearly love the English Shepherd dog. Particularly those who so willingly volunteer so much of their time and effort to promote, protect, and preserve the rich heritage of this fine breed.

Without these people, these selfless dedicated and devoted stalwarts, this ancient breed might well have faded into the annals of canine antiquity.

Thanks to each of you wonderful guys for your loyalty, your commitment, your enthusiasm, and your allegiance.

The United English Shepherd Association[1]
The English Shepherd Club[2]
The American Working Farm Collie Association[3]
The National English Shepherd Rescue League[4]

Preface

When I was a wee lad, had I said to my grandma that dogs like old Shep might someday become a rare sight around the neighborhood, she might have quipped that I was doggone crazy.

A reminder today of just how popular the English Shepherd, or *Farm Collie*, had become during the first half of the twentieth century. Most small farms had at least one or two, and the familiar shepherd could be found around most small town neighborhoods.

Whether bringing home the cows on the farm, or hanging with the kids at the baseball field in town, old Shep was as much a part of Americana as apple pie and Model A's.

I can well remember the trust my parents had in old Shep. Mom thought nothing of running downtown for a few grocery items while leaving my brother Jack (age 5) and me (age 4) in the care of Shep. There was just no way either Jack or I could get out of the yard while Shep was on duty. Our old friend was very casual about "herding" us within the confines of the yard. Actually there were times when Shep would grab us by the seat of the pants and pull us back into the limits of the yard.

When he wasn't herding kids or playing ball with us, he was content to sit on the front porch and stand sentry duty. He would actually be passing judgment on all comers to the home. That was his job. Watch the kids and guard the home. And, no one ever doubted his ability to perform his duties with style and grace. Shep was the sort of guy one could easily take for granted and he never expected anything more. A pat on the head was his reward, along with the occasional outing with the family which meant a ride in the old Oldsmobile.

❧

Background and History
Of the English Shepherd

Because most people are unfamiliar with the English Shepherd, a mention of the dog's breed name will elicit only a puzzled response from most inquirers. The obvious is usually a look of: "I think I know, but give me a hint" kind of quandary.

Such puzzlement is quite normal since most equate the English Shepherd dog with perhaps the Old English Sheep Dog, the English Springer Spaniel, or the English Setter. Most are not quite sure.

Of course, if you refer to your dog as just a "Farm Collie" you might get some sense of recognition. Like: "Oh yeah".

Actually there are a couple of theories about how the name came about. Perhaps the most reasonable explanation is simply that the breed originated in Northern England and throughout Scotland. These dogs, it is believed, are a direct descendant of the cattle dogs brought to the British Isles by the Romans.

From the looks of old photos dating back to the earliest records in North America, the early American farm collies very much resembled those herding dogs in Great Britain. Although these dogs varied in size and coloring, they remained true to type of the old Roman Cattle dogs.

There is also a theory that it was the Amish who inadvertently titled the breed. It is customary for the Amish to refer to anyone outside of their community as: "The English". Therefore; the local farm dogs in the area, other than their own, were referred to as "The English Shepherds".

Early in the twentieth century, there was a growing interest in formal breed registries and it is believed that it was during this period that both the rough collie, sometimes actually called the Scotch Collie, and the Border Collie began to immerge in popularity. Some thought has been given to the belief that both of these breeds were a direct result of selective breeding of the old farm collie stock.

Although the Rough Collie has primarily evolved into a "show dog", the English Shepherd continues primary as a more versatile upright, loose-eyed herding dog with hunting and guarding aptitudes also added to his itinerary.

Cousin to the English Shepherd is the Border Collie, who sports a more concentrated crouching, eye-contact herding style. This breed's performance style is much more animated than the English Shepherd. Although still a working dog, in many cases the Border Collie is increasingly also becoming a show dog.

The most distinctive difference between the English Shepherd and the Border Collie is the obvious "off switch" belonging to the former.

This "off switch" creates a much less aggressive and animated dog both at home and in the field. Many prefer the English Shepherd breed simply because of its gentle temperament which tends to make him a much more adaptable family pet, children's companion, and loyal guardian.

It was just after the Second World War that the English Shepherd breed began to all but disappear from the agricultural scene. Thankfully, the United Kennel Club[5] had the foresight to establish and maintained a breed registry that began in 1927. It was the UKC who first recognized the need to document the pedigree of this most American dog. A dog brought to this country by the first settlers and one who migrated with the settlers West. It was both the English Shepherd along with his other cousin, the Australian Shepherd, who descended from the bloodlines of the old North American farm collie.

With the changing of farming practices during the late nineteen-forties, when more and more dairy cattle rarely went to pasture, and were now pretty much confined to free-style barns and feedlots, the need for a herding shepherd dog began to diminish. It was during this period that the popularity of more stylish dogs began to emerge.

During the early 1940's an English Cocker Spaniel won Best of Show at the Westminster Dog Show. This event drew a great deal of attention to the breed. It became the stylish dog to be seen with, and the race was on to fulfill the demand for this breed's puppies.

There is some consensus that it was the Cocker Spaniel breed that created the incentive for the first lucrative "puppy mills" to follow. It was also the beginning of a trend. That is, how best to create a canine monster by mass producing puppies regardless of sound breeding principals.

In order to accommodate the demand for the puppies, mass inbreeding practices flourished. Doggy incest became the key to abundant profits in the pet kingdom. In short order, greedy kennel operators were producing a strain of dogs flawed with nervous dispositions and some very serious medical problems.

And, so it was the lovable Cocker Spaniel who first began to satisfy America's need for the trendy breeds. For many years to follow it appeared that whatever dog won the Westminster's Best in Show, also won the hearts of the American pet buying public. The Toy Poodle, the Pug, the Chihuahua, the Corgi, the German Shepherd, and most recently, the Labs and Retrievers followed.

Today; the English Shepherd, who actually is not bred for showy looks, but rather is a true performance dog, is making a remarkable comeback. Perhaps nostalgia for the good old North American dog has become contagious.

As more and more old timers sing the praises about the "lassie dogs of yesteryear," the one's they remember as a youth—along with all the myths and legends attached to the dog's prowess—the more popular becomes America's generic dog...the English Shepherd.

Not only the dog that brought home the cows from the pastures for milking every morning and evening, but the dog who supplemented stew meat for the table by helping the family's squirrel hunters during the depression years. A versatile fellow, he also played ball with the kids when off–duty and faithfully guarded the family homestead at all times. As more and more families today realize the value of having an even-tempered, highly intelligent, and happy companion about the home, the more popular the choice becomes for "lassie" to come home.

Why You Should Choose
An English Shepherd Puppy

To begin with, as we have already indicated, perhaps the most popular breed may not be the best choice to introduce into your home as a family pet.

We are all aware that some dog breeds represent status for some. Big city ghettos are populated with Pit Bulls that are intended, I suppose, to make a definite statement about their macho owners. One might make the case that the Toy Poodle also makes a statement for their owners.

And, there are the novelty dogs, the hairless, and the bark less, along with the sled dogs and the coach dogs. Certainly the latter two were not bred to snooze on your couch.

There is the whole line of hunting dogs that are restless and uncomfortable in the home. These dogs have been bred for hundreds of years as kennel dogs. The kennel hounds whose only purpose in life is to run the fox, the rabbit, and the coon. These dogs are capable of running for miles and will track their prey for hours. It strikes me as incredulous to even consider exercising a Beagle or a Bassett with a walk around the block. Almost like asking a weight lifter to work out with a rolling pin.

Then there are the coach dogs to consider. I once had a neighbor who decided to bring home a Dalmatian pup. He was quite proud of the comments the dog would illicit when he walked about the neighborhood with this uniquely spotted dog.

Of course, as the dog matured, he became a pacing, barking fiend. Actually, the dog became a total annoyance for the entire neighborhood. What my friend had never considered was that, although his dog brought him many admiring comments, his Dalmatian was bred to run beneath or alongside of a coach for hours with almost unlimited endurance. Again, a walk around the block just didn't satisfy the dogs inherit need to burn off his almost endless energy.

By contrast, the English Shepherd has been a true family member for centuries. Whether sleeping by the fireside in the shepherd's cottage, or dozing under the Shepherd's chuck wagon, the Farm Collie has always enjoyed a very close relationship with the family, the master, and the mistress.

In essence, in order to do his job, these farm dogs had to be in close communication with the boss. Sometimes, while driving stock, the dog(s) has to be in immediate touch with the boss at all times. Listening, watching, and reacting in a coordinated effort to engage in a symbiotic understanding of mutual communication. To watch a good herding dog in action is without doubt the quintessential act of the dog's ability to bond with man. In the meadow, they are one with the other. The dog's aptitude for reacting immediately to both sight and sound signals from the shepherd is nothing short of astounding.

To better offer an understanding of the intelligence of the English Shepherd dog lets for a moment compare what is required of this breed in order for her to function proficiently. Understandable, the Seeing Eye, and the K9 dogs function far beyond the limits of most Poodles and Pomeranians, let's just for a moment begin to imagine also the demands placed on the good herding dog.

Two important rules of civility which are hard and fast are already ingrained within the psyche of the English Shepherd dog through centuries of breeding these companion dogs.

The first rule within the psyche of the English Shepherd dog is the Rule of Boundary. This rule simply means the dog is to remain outside the boundaries designated by the shepherd. The dog must respect the boundaries designated by the shepherd so the sheep are free to do whatever they want inside their boundaries. The dog is free to do whatever he wants to do outside the boundaries, and the shepherd is free from having to shout commands to his dog which only disrupts the sheep.

Simply put, one of the strong points of the English Shepherd is he knows his place and his limits in the relationship between man and beast.

The second rule of canine civility is to know and understand his place in the pack order.

The "pack order" is the social hierarchy of the shepherd dog's world. Normally, the order would consist of the shepherd, the dog, and the sheep in that order. The three entities form the "working family".

In "pack parlance", the shepherd is the leader; the dog is second in prestige with the authority to act on behalf of the shepherd at all times in accordance with the rules of boundary. The sheep; which today in many cases mean other family members to the dog, are subordinate members of the pack to be protected and watched over at all times.

To best appreciate the intelligence of the English Shepherd and the complexity of communications a herding dog must immediately respond to, lets briefly look at *some of the vocabulary* the herding dog must not only understand, but must react to with uncanny immediacy. In the field either by voice, hand signal or whistle command (or any combination thereof) the dog will respond to:

- Come by (go left)   you're too near, get out
- Away to me (go right)   you're too far, come in
- Lie down   This one (shed this sheep)
- Stand and hold it   Pause

- Go back   Stop, abandon
- Walk onto your sheep   Steady
- On your feet   Walk on
- Look back   That'll do

The shepherd can tell his dog whether he wants him to stop and stay, or stop but get back up again. He can tell the dog to go left or go right a little, go left or right a lot, go left or right slowly, or go left or right now.

And, what seems to be so totally amazing is the concentrated focus on the part of the dog.

So with this in mind, I say again, why choose the English Shepherd breed for your family's companion?

For my part, I can only say that I do not suffer fools gladly. I am a cranky old man. I have no patience with stupid dogs, or stupid anything for that matter. I can't imagine anything more frustrating than dealing with a raucous, vulgar unreachable animal that makes it possible to frustrate your every attempt to civilize a brainless irascible cur.

Whenever I have the occasion to meet an English Shepherd only one thought leaps to my mind. *How incredibly happy this dog truly is.*

With all the griping, complaining, carping, grousing and grumbling going on about us today, I am always pleased to see there is someone or something that is so terrifically, contagiously, inherently happy. And, boy is that ever the case with the English Shepherd. One couldn't find a happier dog than this. This breed is on a permanent high for happiness. It truly is the one best word to describe the English Shepherd. *Happy!*

Andy Rooney of 60 Minutes fame once said: "The average dog is a much nicer person that the average person." I think of this quote most every time one of my dogs comes to greet me. Tail wagging, eyes sparkling, feet dancing and it all represents my canine friend's concept of a standing ovation each time he greets me. How perfectly unrestrained is his attitude of merriment, elation and delight. And just think; it is all motivated by just your appearance and your presence.

And, that dear friend is a treasure not found on the open market. A love for you so completely unalloyed, so absolute, so infallible that only a dancing expression of merriment, jollity, and gaiety will demonstrate how completely you are loved and adored by this ecstatic animal. This devoted pal who will go on excitedly with ecstasy and rapture to make the point.

In short, if one considers the breed's high caliber of intelligence combined with his loving affection and easy compatibility it makes for an obvious match when you choose an English Shepherd.

The Breed's Appearance And Standards

There are five predominant colors, and color patterns present in the typical English Shepherd which are:

1) Black and tan
2) Tri-color, which is black, tan, and white
3) Black and white
4) Sable and white
5) Tan and White[6]

A sable dog's coloring may vary from a pale honey-gold color through a deep mahogany coat. The sable may have black-tipped hairs, or may have a solid black saddle pattern. It is also possible to appear as a clear blonde honey color without black pigment in the coat.

White coloring is typically either full or partial collar along with white socks or stockings. A black mask is acceptable in any of the color patters with or without a white collar.

Splotchy white patterns covering more than 30 percent of the body are never permitted in any of the color patterns. Solid white coats or piebald markings are an undesirable trait. It should be noted that *Merles do not appear* in the English Shepherd breed.[7]

Hundreds of years of breeding have produced an all-purpose dog. Contented in both rural and urban environments, today's English Shepherd has evolved into the all-around family pet.

Although their past responsibilities have ranged from herding, protecting livestock, vermin control, guarding the home, hunting squirrel and rabbit as well as watching over the children, the past versatilities of the breed have all contributed toward perfecting this dog as a well-mannered companion.

Of medium size and balance proportion, the dog stands 18 to 26 inches at the shoulder, and will weigh between 35 to 80 pounds. Males are usually larger than females.

Unlike the Rough Collie, the English Shepherd's nose (muzzle) is moderately broad, neither pugged nor pointed.

Eyes are brown and should express character and alertness. Ears should be set wide apart, slightly erect at the base and close to the head when relaxed.

The coat of the dog is of medium length and texture, and is acceptable straight, wavy or curly with an undercoat that sheds seasonally. The bitch will have a greater tendency for shedding than the male.

The tail is plumed, and forelegs are moderately feathered. *The coat of these dogs should require only limited grooming.*

The true appeal of these dogs is their even temperament and gentle disposition along with their high degree of intelligence. Combined with their athleticism and trainability, they excel in many modern day activities such as obedience and agility competition. Their versatility extends to Search and Rescue and many have become certified Therapy Dogs.

Primarily a very healthy breed, their average lifespan is between 13 to 15 years, although I have owned several who have survived to the ripe old age of nineteen.

Where to Find English Shepherd Puppies?

The English Shepherd dog, as I have said earlier, is a rare breed. Rare in the sense that I mean hard to find or scarce. Of course, they are also rare in the sense of being unique or matchless in the character and compatibility, but in this instance I mean the former.

I have ransacked Google and the Internet trying to get a fix on the number of English Shepherd breeders in the US. It seems that no amount of searching will account for more than 40 to 50 *active breeders* throughout the Continental US. And, much to my surprise, it is even more difficult to find breeders in Canada on the Web. Perhaps this is a further indication that here is truly the good old American dog.

Of course, there are more than likely a number of English Shepherd breeders who do not frequent the Internet. However; I would imagine that today, with so much economic activity centered on the Web, along with its ease of access, only a very small minority would not focus their business efforts here. Or, at least become a listed breeder along with others with one of the major breeder clubs.

Even though most of my puppy sales are local, without my web page I am sure it would be difficult to introduce buyers to the breed. And, even more difficult for me to convincing prospective buyers of the breed's value as both a pet and a companion within the scope of just a simple classified advertisement. My classified advertising may arouse the curiosity of the buyer, but it is certainly my web pages that close the sale.

If you are having difficulty locating a puppy, I suggest you go to the web and search for a breeder with a litter for sale.

There, your primary sources are likely to be one of the English Shepherd clubs or associations. The main ones are going to be:

- The United English Shepherd Association
- The English Shepherd Club
- The American Farm Collie Association.

You might also try: The National English Shepherd Rescue League if you are interested in finding a mature dog, or are willing to help find a home for an abandoned dog. Sometimes they even have an occasional puppy for adoption. This group also features a web site–http://www.nesr.org on the Internet. Any of the above groups are easily accessed though a Google search. I don't believe there is an implied endorsement of the breeders they list; however, it is certainly a good place to start in your search for your pup.

Selective a Proper Pup

Unlike many other purebreds, the English Shepherd has *never* been bred exclusively for the show ring. Therefore; because these dogs have been bred primarily for their working style and capability, and never for show ring qualities, there are a few characteristics you should look for and other traits you should try to avoid when selecting your pup?

First off, as mentioned before, the English Shepherd has a couple of close relatives in the *Border Collie* and *Australian Shepherd* family line. Both these breeds are often confused with the English Shepherd; and in fact, are no doubt the *better known* of the herding breeds.

Unlike the English Shepherd both of these other breeds are recognized by the American Kennel Club (AKC). Some of these *others* are bred for the show ring and not for their working or inherent shepherding abilities.

One of the primary characteristics about both of these *other* shepherd dogs is that they display a much more aggressive tendency in their working styles.

Actually, the *Australian Shepherd* breed was developed primarily in the Western US during the 19th and 20th centuries as a ranch dog. In many cases they were used to herd or handle horses. Wrangling horses obviously requires a much more aggressive approach to herding. Meaning a more determined and assertive initiative that would be lacking in the gentler nature of the English Shepherd. The latter is more of a sheep, cattle, and poultry type of herding dog.

The *Australian Shepherd* like the English Shepherd works in an upright position and is also a loose-eyed herding dog. The "Aussie" can further be distinguished from most other herding dogs by their usually stubby tail. Coloring also sets this breed apart from the English Shepherd. The *Australian Shepherds* have two basic colors both red and black. Essentially, the blue merle is a black dog carrying the merling gene and the red merle is a red dog also carrying the merling gene.

During the *Australian Shepherd's* development its usual work included moving very large herds of sheep and cattle from summer to winter grazing grounds and back. Their work also involved flushing range cattle out of heavy brush, and moving livestock in tight quarters such as chutes and alleys. These jobs are still where Australian Shepherds excels and are most valued. Obviously, this type of work always requires a more aggressive attitude toward handling livestock. This dog subsequently demonstrates a very positive initiative and an assertive nature.

The *Border Collie* significantly differs from either the *English Shepherd* or the *Australian Shepherd* by nature and its working style. The Border Collie is defined as a fixed-eyed herding dog. You can't mistake the "eye" of a Border Collie for its intense gaze and focus. They work with head low to the ground, hindquarters high and tail tucked between their hind legs. Their coloring presents a variety similar to the Aussie, including merles. Apart from reds and lilac's they also appear in half-white face varieties.

The *Border Collie* also has a tendency to "clap" or go down and face the sheep with its belly close to the ground. This, in combination with "eye", gives the Border Collie a singularly predatory look. These dogs have been bred for "clapping" and "strong eye" for many years and it is a very distinguishing characteristic.

It is a mistake many people make in selecting a *Border Collie* as a home companion. This dog needs work every day *without exception*. Either you must offer the dog a job to do every day, or he will find one. Perhaps it will be one not to your liking either. They are an exceptional active dog and are bred to run and chase for long hours every day. Rarely do they display a liking for the home and hearth.

The *Australian Shepherd* is a somewhat of a less active and demanding dog, although again, these dogs would prefer some sort of activity.

Which brings us back to the English Shepherd and what to look for in a pup? Unlike the other Shepherd types, this Shepherd has an "off switch". An affectionate term used among the breed's lovers to define one of its most positive characteristics. These dogs also love to work, to run and to frolic. And, they do make excellent herding dogs. However, most are contended to sit by the feet of the mistress at day's end, and enjoy the more simple pleasures of dogdom's idea of snooze and relax.

Before we get into the ideals of selecting a puppy, let's consider an important aspect of dog ownership. You have got to like (love) this dog for a lot of years to come.

So, the first rule is: Don't settle! If; as a child, you had always dreamed of a cream-colored pony for endless days and nights, it would logically follow that the likes and love of a bay colored pony would soon diminish.

So, if you have looked over the field of color choices in the English Shepherd, and you have decided you like the Tri-color dogs, don't settle on a light sable just because that is all there is available for the moment. Hesitate long enough to make your dreams come true. Both you and the dog will be thankful you waited.

The second rule is: Check out the breeder. *By no means buy a pup from a pet store.* Is that an unfair condemnation? Not at all. It is fair because by all that is holy it is an absolute just assessment of a very bad circumstance.

Pups that get dumped in a pet store are those coming from a mass production facility. You will never convince me that a responsible breeder with a conscience and a love for animals would arbitrarily offload his dogs to anonymous buyers without regard for their future. Pet store pups come from puppy mills.

Otherwise; why would I, as a responsible breeder, accept less than half the actual value of the pup unless it was to create volume profits? You might rightfully conclude that volume puppies mature into less than ideal dogs?

No, if I carefully select good breeding stock and abide by all the rules of prudent care and maintenance, I am going to make darned sure my pups go to responsible and loving families.

And, further, I will more than likely license my kennel so that I will be accredited by responsible government authorities leaving little doubt of my concern for prospective buyers, and for the puppies I sell.

How does one evaluate a responsible breeder who kennels quality dogs with loving care?

Well, again there exist in most States a Department of Agriculture and Markets who sort of regulate dog breeders and kennels. This means that in most cases at least once a year someone from the Department actually visits the kennel facilities and decides whether or not the owner is doing a reasonable job of caring for the animals, and not just taking advantage of the dam's ability to produce litters.

Then today, of course, there is the Internet. What better way of comparing and contrasting available litters than to get on the World Wide Web and shop for the puppy of your dreams? And, by all means, ask for references.

There are going to be a few responsible breeders who for one reason or another do not have a web site. But, for the most part, you will be able to locate a reasonable assortment of breeders on the web with available litters who will be more than willing to present their bona fides and credentials.

There will be instances when you may have to ship your puppy. If there are no local breeders, or none with available litters, then your next decision will be whether or not to have your puppy flown to you via an available airline.

This venture offers a much wider selection of puppies to choose from, and is a reasonably safe and easy means of obtaining the dog you really want. Of course, there is an added expense that will run anywhere from $250 and up to the cost of your puppy. The airline will demand not only an approved shipping crate, but also a Bill of Health from a certified veterinarian. A certified Veterinarian meaning one who is endorsed by the U.S. Department of Agriculture giving special meaning to term "certified."

An out of State or out of Town breeder also means you will have to establish complete confidence in the breeder's description of the pups in the litter. Here is where the liaison becomes a mere matter of faith. You can look at the photos of the pups, but you must rely on the good faith of the breeder to accurately describe the dog she is sending to you.

If, however, you can make an on the spot inspection of the entire litter locally, then you must have some idea of what it is you are looking for.

In the old days there was a technique followed to determine the more aggressive pups in the litter. Supposedly, when you arrived on the site of the breeder's kennel, you should create some sort of loud diversion. Clap your hands or shout. Any means necessary to startle the pups. Those pups that would scatter and cringe from the sound would supposedly be those less desirable dogs for future training.

I have always questioned this method of selection and sometimes believe it is more myth than reality. I am certain that employing this devise for puppy selection would more than likely unnecessarily negate a whole lot of very suitable candidates who would otherwise become ideal lifelong companions.

Believe it or not, even as an experienced breeder, for the most part I still go by gut feelings.

Not necessarily choosing the friendly little pup who first rushes to greet me. Or, for that matter, the one who surprisingly likes to hang out at my feet while I am talking with the breeder. This method of selection would mean something similar to that silly rationalization that: "the pup choose me".

Allowing the pup to chose would certainly absolve you of any responsibility for things to come.

I like to spend time just observing the interplay and interaction of the pups in their home environment. It is surprising how much symbiosis one can conger just by observing how pups react to one another and to visiting strangers.

When I say "gut feeling" that is really all there is to go on given a few perimeters to also consider.

Try to picture sometime in the future what this puppy will become. And, in conjunction with that thought, what type of companionship you have idealized for this *future* dog. I suppose that everyone thinks immediately, while surveying the litter, they would like the most "outgoing" pup. If we are to equate "outgoing" with dominance, then just assume that now, and in the future, this pup may continue to challenge *you* for the position of Alpha dog in the home pack.

That's exactly right. Challenge you now and again to be *top dog*. I suppose you have heard of *problem* dogs. Although there can be many different diagnosis for problem dogs, one such is the continuing aspiration of your dog to dominate...even *you*.

(There are some authorities who dispute this theory of "Alpha Dog" even exist in the home environment.[8] As a lifetime owner and observer of multi-dog packs, continual Alpha challenges appear both obvious and ordinary to me.)

Therefore; play your hunches when considering a future pup. Do you really want the most dominate pup in the litter? Think for a moment about the other end of the spectrum. How about the shy, retiring guy?

I have known cases where this guy makes for the perfect match. Maybe you are looking for a pooch who would be contented to spend time by himself. The sort of guy who would prefer *not to be challenged* by others. If you are a person who spends long hours away from home perhaps a more reticent, quiet sort of guy might fit the bill. A dog who feels challenged by everyone but you, feels comfortable only with you. Not a bad deal for the single person looking for quiet companionship.

On the other hand, if you are looking for a working dog; a dog for either herding or agility contest, or you have a family of rowdy, raucous kids, you might want to look for a more domineering fellow who can mingle and hold his own in the fray.

There is another factor to consider while at the breeder's kennel discovering the right puppy for you. Although a pup may be perfectly adjusted to life in his currently family situation with mom and siblings, you might ask the breeder to separating him to a new and different environment away from the others and test his reaction. Here, you'll be the judge. How does he handle strange circumstances?

Then there is the old controversy about gender. What makes the better pet? Is it the male or the female that is best suited for a family pet? Let's first review all the old myths about the genders. Girls are smarter, less dominate, and don't wander like boys. If you choose to believe all of the above you are fifty percent correct. I have never been able to generalize about whom or what makes the better choice.

I have always owned multiple dogs (packs) and have never been able to predict personalities. I have owned some females who won't stay home, some males far more loving and affectionate than females and dumb dogs in both genders. Again, look over the prospects and go with your gut.

However; there are some special considerations when deciding on whether to choose a male or female. Males are usually larger and cost less to neuter. Unless you plan to breed your dog, spay or neuter is the way to go. Forget that nonsense about spaying makes them fat and listless. Too much food and little exercise makes them fat and listless.

Also that old saw about letting them have one litter before spaying is the equivalent of giving them one shot at a genital type of cancer. And, one more thing. If you can't afford the surgery, you can't afford the dog.

Spayed females have fewer tendencies to contract mammary or uterine cancer or uterine infections. Castrated males have less risk of testicular cancer, and neutering reduces their need to mark their territory. It also limits their territory because they won't have an irrepressible desire to wonder off looking for girlfriends. (They can smell a girl friend as far as four miles off.)

Much of your future happiness with this puppy is going to depend a whole lot on the honesty of the breeder. You should put every bit as much effort into selecting the breeder you purchase from as you do in choosing the pup.

You should absolutely demand the pup's certificate of health signed by a veterinarian. This certificate should also designate a vaccine record, along with worming medicine administered and the results of the physical examination.

You might further ask if the parents have been OFA'ed. (Orthopedic Foundation for Animals) which is a non-profit group that will analyze the hip and socket joint x-rays provided to them by a certified animal clinic.

The dog must be two years old to qualify for certification. The condition may be either inherited or the result of a traumatic articular fracture of the joint. It is a costly procedure and obviously will add significantly to the price of the offspring. *It does not, however, offer any guarantee* that the offspring will be free of the disability, or will not suffer this form of arthritis in the future.

You should also have some guarantee that you will be able to return the puppy should there be some legitimate reason for doing so.

It is important to see one or both parents to gage the temperament and personality of the mom or dad. In many States, licensed kennels have mandatory guidelines for return policies.

Bringing Home Puppy

First, we should consider at what age is the puppy ready to go home with you.

Puppies open their eyes when they are about two weeks old. When they about three weeks old they begin to hear. It isn't until they are about four weeks old that they can move around pretty well. So up until now, mom is just a snuggly warming source and a drink of milk.

It is about the ripe old age of four weeks that the pups begin exploring their environment. They will now begin playing with toys and engaging in mock battles with their siblings. If weaned at five or six weeks and shipped to a pet store with so little time to spend with mom and their mates, it is difficult to imagine being *immature* at this tender young age. More than likely such a pup will suffer antisocial behavior for the remainder of his life.

On the other hand, there is an excellent book on the subject of allowing mom the opportunity of bringing up puppy. "Mother Knows Best"[9] is a theory that the dog is a social animal and mother is the most successful teacher.

If you have ever had the chance to observe Mom with her litter, you will understand what the author is talking about. Mom suffers no nonsense from her brood and disciplines accordingly. The pups are first exposed to a regimen of socialization by their interchanges with their mother. They learn both excess' and limitations in their early weeks with mom as their teacher. So, understandably, it is best to leave the brood intact until they reach at least seven to eight weeks of age.

It is also important to understand that just the interplay with their siblings creates an unmistakable lesson on how hard to bite before repercussions follow.

Next, let's make a list of what you will need to make puppy's adjustment in his new home as stress-free as possible.

Along with the pup, you should take home with you a sampling of the food that he has been eating at the breeder's kennel. You really should adjust his diet to a change in foods as gradual as possible. The poor guy will have enough stress to deal with, and mealtime should be the least of his worries.

Also, you should have a towel or a blanket with you that you can rub over mom, and possibly some of his littermates, so that you can take home with you the sense of smell that will later offer comfort and well-being to the pup in his new surroundings.

A crate for your new pup should not only become an essential part of his training, but should also represent a cozy sanctuary for him to feel secluded and secure. You can purchase an adult size crate for your puppy now and adapt it to his current use by blocking off a portion with a cardboard box leaving him just enough room to comfortably stand, turn about, and lie down. In this way, there will be no need to purchase a larger crate as your pup grows.

There is the obvious inventory of things to have ready including: feeding dishes, water bowls, chew toys, collars, and leashes. Remember the smelly towel or blanket you brought home from the breeders? The one you rubbed on mom and the siblings? That goes in the crate.

By way of leashes, there is a new device available called the Gentle Leader which is a headcollar available on line. Not to be used on a puppy before he is eight to ten weeks old, the Gentle Leader is a different approach that helps to prevent pulling, lunging, jumping, and all those bad habits a pup learns before walking nicely on a lead. My Shepherds like it. It makes for a quick and easy approach to kinder and gentler dog walking.

Puppy Training

The first anxiety you will experience upon bringing a new puppy into your home is the dilemma of "housebreaking". The easiest approach to training your new puppy potty manners is the use of a crate[10] to contain him when you can't be watching.

The crate training approach is far and away the simplest means of dealing with this age old problem. It goes without saying that the old approach of using newspapers...both to pee upon, and rolled up for spanking...is passé and harmful to both man and beast.

For the sake of Puppy, it is important to remember that a he has little bladder or sphincter control when he is less than four months of age (16 weeks). Younger pups have even less control and normally have to eliminate as frequently as eight to twelve times a day.

That said, I have repeatedly heard feedback from my buyers of English Shepherd pups reporting that they are most precocious when it comes to potty training. Many of my pups, with the exception of an occasional accident, are pretty well trained at nine or ten weeks old. *Such an achievement does require the pup is escorted outside at regular and frequent intervals.*

Here are the simple rules (absolute) for crate training:

Never use the crate as a punishment for your puppy. He should always feel comfortable and secure while in the privacy of *his den.*

Let the puppy *discover* his crate. Find a spot either in your bedroom *(best)*, kitchen, or wherever is going to be his permanent home place for the crate. Place the "smelly towel" or blanket in the crate along with a nice tasty treat. Here is the important part. Don't try to imprison him in the crate immediately, but try to allow him to enter and leave several times before closing him into his new home.

If you are patient and allow this new adventure to be fun for the pup, you will be rewarding with less whining and yipping when you eventually have to leave him for the night. At first, leave him in the crate for only a few moments, and then reward him with a treat and loving praise before his release. Slowly, but very, very slowly increase the time you leave the pup in the crate.

Never open the door to the crate while he is crying even if it means waiting for an extended interval. If he associates whining with getting the door to open you know you are just asking for trouble.

Take him outside before putting him in the crate for any extended period of time.

Never punish him for a mistake or an accident. You may relieve your frustration while cleaning up a mess by scolding him, but the pup at this age will have no idea what he is being punished for. Remember, biologically he has little control over his bladder or sphincter at this young age.

Take him outside *immediately* upon leaving the crate. For the first few days it is best to carry him outside to insure he doesn't have an accident on the way out. And remember you can never overdo the amount of praise you offer the pup once he has relieved himself on the proper spot.

Make sure the crate is not placed near a heat outlet or in direct sunlight.

The crate training approach is based on the principal that *"mom"* at some point in the pup's development has disciplined him for relieving himself in the *"nest"*. The pup has learned that he should never *go* in the *nest*, but must travel outside to *go*. *Outside*, to a pup, is the next most convenient spot. That is why it is important to carry the pup all the way outside at first.

A couple of other hints may help. Animals are truly creatures of habit. They love a schedule so if you provide them with a regular timetable, they will almost go on demand.

You might also control her intake to some degree. A pup's digestion is predicable. Shortly after in, is out. And, once you learn to observe your pup's signals, you will be able to predict when it is time to go out. Sniffing and scouting should tell you the obvious. She has to go.

I have found that having an older well trained dog in the home along with the pup is a big help with early training. It seems that the pup will follow along with his senior. Of course, I always make it a point to let "senior" out more often than usual so that the pup gets the idea of where the latrine is–and where it is not—very quickly.

A word about *come, sit and stay*. These three basic lessons will surely come in handy if you can teach your pup to obey them. *In fact, it is very difficult to not have these three commands at hand when certain situations arise with your pup.*

I'll let you in on a very valuable confidentiality. The secret to successful dog training is most elementary. This secret has been kept concealed and private for years by professional dog handlers.

However; I can put you on the road to master dog handler with just two words. *Have fun.*

That's right. It never fails. That's really all there is to it. If for any reason you are not in the mood. If you are still; in your mind, muttering about that creepy idiot boss of yours, or your brother-in-law overstaying his welcome, or that nosy neighbor bitch next door, or why do I always have to clean up the dog poop...don't even think about a training session with your pup. Let it go until you are in a more positive frame of mind.

Just having fun with your pup can be very educational for the both of you. How much faster a training session will go if you are inclined to make it a fun event. A pup will learn his lesson sooner if he suspects that you are pleased with him. And conversely, you will be in a much more suitable frame of mind if you are pleased with yourself. So the first rule of puppy training is: *Have fun.*

There is a recent hypothesis among dog training that speculates dogs are merely operant learners.[11] This supposition means they respond to, or obey our commands by way of an action or a behavior that does not appear to have a stimulus?

While training puppy we must bear in mind that he lives exclusively in the present. He has little or no concept of the past, nor can he conceptualize his future. He does not understand language, although somehow he is able to discriminate the relevance of certain of our vocal sounds.

If he does respond to certain reoccurring situations, it is more likely attributed to an instinctual impulse rather than a thought process involving memories of past experiences.

In order for a dog to respond to any form of training, the owner must first realize that his dog only learns from the *immediate results* of his actions. Only those events occurring closely together in time will bear any meaning for the student. It is a concept you must focus upon and always be committed to which means when your dog responds correctly, your reward should become an immediate reflex action.

All of your training efforts will go for naught unless you truly appreciate this one absolute—completely and unequivocally–that waiting longer than just a few seconds will confuse your dog and he will not be able to associate the reward with the appropriate behavior.

This accounts for the current fascination with the idea of "clicker training".[12]

The clicker is that little hand held metal devise operated with the thumb and forefinger. It offers your dog an immediate response. It becomes a subliminal signal that a treat or high praise will follow.

The idea is to sound a forewarning that a treat is forthcoming. Immediacy is the reason for the clicker. When we say that your dog responds to training thru immediate results, we really mean *immediate.*

How often when I have tried to use food treats to motivate one of my dogs during a training session I have been unable to get the reward to him as soon as he responds. The problem is I would have to be completely ambidextrous in order to satisfy the immediacy requirement of the reward.

That is where the clicker comes in. The clicker tells him he has succeeded and a reward is forthcoming.

In short, it is an "event marker", according to Ogden Lindsley, Ph.D. The clicker noise is a conditioned reinforcer that bridges the time that elapses between earning the reward and receiving he reward.

The click also ends the behavior. You are telling your dog that not only is it a job well done, but the job *is* done.

Now that we understand a little more about how a dog learns, let me tell you how easy it is to teach the three basic commands. Sit, Stay and Come.

The lesson for *sit* is easy enough. Simply ask the dog to *sit* while applying slight pressure on his back side and perhaps simultaneously offering a treat hoisted above and behind his nose. When he arrives at the *sit* position, you should just go ballistic with praise.

Make a fuss. Let him know beyond any doubt that he is the best, most intelligent dog in all of creation. Your dog will absolutely demonstrate to you that he is happiest when you are happy. He is most pleased whenever he can please you. So don't hold back. Demonstrate your pleasure with the little successes your dog might have.

The sit command for your dog is comparable to the "Attention" command demanded of all those dog faces in the U.S. Military. Having once been one of those "dog faces" in the 82nd Airborne Division, I learned that before any other command was given, we were first called to "Attention". Then a sequence of commands was offered.

Similarly, it is best to require (command) your dog to "sit" first before any sequential command is offered.

Come should be easier yet for your pup to understand. If your dog won't *come* to you when you call, then you have disobeyed the first rule of dog handling. Simply, you are not demonstrating happiness when you are training. If, for instance, each time your puppy approaches you, you demonstrate just how happy you are to see him, then he should never hesitate to *come* to you.

If need be, there is the long rope technique. Take your pup to an open area, along with your clicker, a rope, and a pocket full of treats. Ask her to sit, and then retreat a few yards from her. Now, call her and gently tug a bit on the rope. Once she responds and approaches, offer her a click, and then a treat from your pocket.

Gradually, she will associate the command (either "come" or "her name") with the click and finally the treat.

How about the command: Stay? This is a little more difficult for your pup to understand because she is just so in love with you that she hates any form of separation from you. *Stay* requires patience and repetition on your part. Begin by having your pup sit. Then with your palm extended toward her, ask her to *stay* while moving back a step or two. Reward her with praise if she stays. If she doesn't understand... repeat. Again, with patients and repetition along with a great deal of praise for small increments of success, continue until you achieve your goal.

Here's another important note to remember. Only during the early training sessions will you repeat over again the command. Once she has mastered your direction to sit, come, and stay, you should not have to repeat the commands multiple times. If you have to continue to repeat any of these commands in multiples, what it amounts to is that you are offering your dog an option to obey. Be firm and make it clear there are never times when it is ok not to obey.

The English Shepherd is fully capable of responding to commands immediately, so it defeats the purpose of training if you have to coax your dog to behave in a positive and forthright manner.

You must never punish your dog for not obeying a specific command. If you do, you take all the fun out of training. And, your success solely depends on having fun.

I like this newly discovered evidence of an advanced mental ability of dogs that was once thought to be only specific to humans.

This new evidence called "selective imitation" brings new meaning to how dogs can learn specific actions. Here we are finding out that dogs can differentiate between two types of behaviors. One is an act of necessity: I have my hands full right now so I will have to open the door using my elbow. Then, there are acts of inefficient preference: Even though my hands aren't full right now, I will open the door with my elbow anyway. When dogs and infants observe this behavior, they inevitably select the latter.

I think this somewhat bears me out when I tell you have fun with your dog while in training. He loves the goofy you. Not the enforcer, not the stickler, nor the martinet. The silly, wacky, giddy, dippy you is a whole lot less threatening for your guy to understand, and a lot more fun to be around.

It is important to understand that training sessions should be brief at first. Never overstay your welcome with the pups' acceptance to learn. In the beginning a five minute session can become an eternity for a playful pup. Very gradually extend your lesson and rarely consider exceeding ten minutes without a playful recess. And, again always make it fun for both of you.

My English Shepherd pups are always precocious. Usually by the time they are three months old they have mastered the sit, come and stay curriculum.

There are a whole lot of dogs out there that don't get enough exercise or companionship because their owners have not taken the time to teach them to heel. Granted, a dog pulling on the leash, and tugging in all directions makes walking the dog like walking the plank. Nobody readily invites that kind of punishment.

By contrast, what a joy it is to be with your pal on a cool evening's jaunt. A joy when you have little to consider except a remission from your daily concerns. A chance to stretch your legs. You could also walk off a few pounds while in the company of your best friend and enthusiastic admirer.

If you are having real difficulties with leading your dog, you might want to try the Gentle Leader mentioned earlier. Most pet suppliers sell them.

To begin with, collar and leash your dog. Ask him to sit. Then, with the command "heel", start walking at a brisk pace. Now, here is the secret to success. Just as soon as your dog *begins to lead you*, turn on your heel—about face—and proceed in the opposite direction. And, once again, just as soon as your dog *begins to lead you*, counter with a reversal of direction.

It may take a number of repetitions before he gets the idea of what is being demanded of him. It may even take several marching sessions, but before long he will understand and conform to your pace and your position.

In fact, it won't be long before you won't even need the lead. If you offer him enough praise when he obeys and he comes to understand how much you enjoy being with him on these walks, he won't leave your side even for a squirrel darting up a tree nearby. *(Not)*

Here I want to take a break to explain the standard command language. There isn't any. It doesn't really matter whether you tell your dog to "sit", "squat" or "stagger". He doesn't understand the "word"; he learns to associate your "inflection" with a given action. So don't get too hung up on the etiquette of dog language. Use a vocabulary that is most comfortable for you and your dog.

Here is yet another secret to successful dog training. *Do nothing but observe.* Once your dog is caught in the act of doing something cute, or unusual encourage him to repeat whatever it is he is doing. If he is making some sort of sound such as a wine or groan, sing along and play along. Make a fuss and sing, hum, chortle...whatever it takes to encourage your dog to continue and improvise on whatever it is *he* has instigated.

Actually, you don't believe those singing dogs you see on television were trained virtuosos do you? And, most of David Letterman's Stupid Pet Tricks evolved from something originated by the pet and only encouraged and nurtured by the owners.

For example, you want your dog to "play dead'. You must start by encouraging your pup to feel confidant while lying on his back. For animals this is a very unnatural and vulnerable position. They are uneasy in this position because of their vulnerability, so you must begin by assuring the pup that nothing is going to harm him while in this position.

Next, begin by cradling your pup in your arms like a baby while he is small enough to handle. Coo and charm the guy by rubbing his belly and talking soothingly to him. The object here is to give him every reassurance that he is safe in this vulnerable position. There; you are already half way home with teaching him to "play dead". Place him on the floor in a position on his back. Gently, while rubbing his belly, ask him to "Stay" and gradually move away. Again, it will require a lot of patients and repetition, but this is the sort of thing you are going to have to live with if you ever intend to make it on the Letterman show.

This "method" of observation and encouragement is also an important technique to utilize if you decide you want to go further with your dog's education one day.

If you should decide that you want to take advantage of your English Shepherd's unique intelligence to train him for herding; or agility, or just having fun with him at the dog park, then you should begin early when he is yet a puppy.

Obviously we can't go into complete detail now because such training would involve a whole other book. However; if you go back to those initial commands we spoke of earlier, you might want to consider trying a few with your pup. Because it is so important that in a given competition that your dog is able to comprehend both spoken and silent-gesture type commands, think about playing a game with your pet. Actually; a learning session should be short intervals of mutual enjoyment.

Now think about any of those "herding commands" we spoke of earlier. Actually, properly executed these same commands apply equally well to Agility Competitions. "Come by" meaning go left can be taught by facing your pet and throwing a ball to your left. But, instead of hollering "fetch", say "come by" and before you throw the ball raise your left arm–if you are right handed—so your dog can see this gesture, and at the same time offer a *short staccato whistle*.

The key to successful dog training is *repetition, patients and reward*. Dogs, like most animals, are creatures of *habit*. Get your pup accustomed to learning through forming a series of fun-filled *habitual* routines.

To get him in the "away to me" (go right) habit, each time before throwing the ball to the right shout "away to me" while at the same time gesturing (pumping) with your right arm and simultaneously offering a *long low whistle*. The habit of running to his right each time he hears you say "away to me" and associates those spoken words with seeing your raised right arm, along with hearing a *long, low whistle* will soon become ingrained along with the enjoyment of the game.

Here are a couple of more tips. The commands, the gestures, and the whistle tones are not writ in stone. You should personalize them and use whatever makes you comfortable.

If you have difficulty whistling, then improvise. For instance, instead of trying to puff your cheeks for a short staccato whistle, buy a whistle and blow short blasts...or whatever. And, make up whatever silent signal gestures you fancy. Just remember, it doesn't take any longer to teach your pup to obey all three commands...verbal, gesture and whistle signals all at the same time with this method.

And besides it is a lot of fun once you have perfected the moves. I have had many fun sessions with visiting kids pretending that I can predict the movements of one of my dogs.

With me standing behind the children where they can't see me, I sent my dog off. (Cast) As soon as the dog is some distance from us, I remark to the children that the silly dog is going to run to his left, as I casually raise my left arm. And, then "wait, wait, no that silly dog is going to turn around and run right at that tree", as I secretly signal with my right arm. "Oh look, now that dog is tired and is going to lie down", as

I offer yet another silent signal, etc. Kids are continually puzzled about my ability to predict every move that distant dog is going to make.

You get the picture. And, believe me when I tell you that I have owned dozens of English Shepherd dogs and they are all equally smart, alert dogs who love any learning experience you offer. Not only love it, but thrive on it. These happy, clever guys are quick to learn and are always anxious to join with you in the excitement of the game.

In conclusion then, if we are to combine the English Shepherd's innate happiness, unlimited enthusiasm for learning and gifted intelligence there is no doubt in my mind that should you make the choice of this breed you too will enjoy a world of happy, enthusiastic rewards.

Certainly you can go out and purchase a puppy training book. There are, I believe, hundreds on the market. However; you must first understand there are no "miracle books" out there, and frankly while studying most of these tombs mine eyes gloss over.

Later in my glossary I will make a few recommendations regarding some books that might be helpful, but for now I will offer a few simple rules for training puppy.

One of the first things you must understand about the nature of your puppy is that he craves your attention. Absolutely, he will do anything to gain your interest in his world.

Much like a child, if he hears you continually calling his name he will be encouraged to do whatever it is that causes you to refer to him. If you are constantly hollering: "put that down, don't chew on that, bad dog, mustn't do that", boy oh boy are you ever playing into his game. He is differently getting the attention he craves.

Although the Breed is labeled English Shepherd, don't be confused. Like all dogs they don't understand the English language. *Mostly the cure for negative behavior is quite simply exercise.* There is nothing more beneficial for both puppy and owner than a play yard. Along with deciding which puppy to buy, you should at the same time be considering what type of fencing to purchase. A play yard is the solution for all of your frustrations when bringing up puppy.

I dare say some sort of recreational area is essential when considering ownership of a puppy. In the city the dog park or local cemetery, or even the garage when possible, can be your survival sanctuary. In suburbia and beyond, a play yard is a must.

So forget about all the negatives when addressing your puppy. Like the old saw says, it only encourages them. If you begin to understand that puppy doesn't understand the words you utter, he merely comprehends your inflections associated with those familiar utterances. That is truly why those "baby talk" inflections really do work while training your dog. As annoying as they may be to others, your pup loves and encourages them. "Ooooh, you are such a goood puppy!!!" and the likes of which make for good and positive communication with your dog.

Here is another important clue to understand your dog's mind. Shunning is the attitude your dog fears most. As much as he loves your *attention*, conversely the thing he dreads most is your *inattention*. If you really want to make your point with your dog most effectively...merely shun him. Try to compose a situation whereby you can get him within seconds to recognize his bad behavior. The key here is: *get him to recognize his bad behavior first. Then shun him.* This method is a whole lot more effective than shouting a series of negatives at the pup.

Which leads us to the ultimate means of shunning for a dog? Chaining or tying a dog out is the most malicious cruelty you can inflect upon your dog. There is nothing whatsoever as callous or heartless as chaining a dog in the backyard or to the front porch or where ever. If you are curious about the term: "meaner than a junkyard dog", then tie your dog out. If you do, I sincerely hope one day he succeeds in biting a big hole in your leg or better yet...devours you. I can't think of a better reason for justifiable homicide.

If you can't manage to provide a play yard or a means of regular exercise for your dog...than buy a cat.

For example, I have sold dozens of puppies over the years, and the only time a previous buyer calls to inform me their dog has bitten someone is absolutely without exception a case whereby the owner has decided to tie the dog out.

Further, it doesn't matter if the dog's leash is attached to a long cable run. A tied-up dog suffers a miserable existence by himself *shunned* and *abandoned.* This form of restraint defies thousands of years of evolution for the dog. He is a pack animal, and as such, knows his *lone existence* means his ultimate demise. Chained in the backyard to a dog's thinking is the equivalent of being cut-off from the pack. Without the pack the dog knows inherently there is no chance for his survival.

There is one absolute guarantee that can be associated with a tied-up dog. Within a matter of days it is possible to convert a gentle loving dog into a frenzied Freudian beast. And speaking of Freud, if such an owner would chance a little self-analysis, it should be obvious that mentally he has retreated from any original concept of owning a dog. In his mind, he has abandoned his responsibility for the dog when he ties him in the yard.

By contrast, once you bring your eight-week old puppy home you must begin the socialization count-down. You have approximately another eight weeks to acclimate the guy to the world of humans and other creatures. Do you know why dogs bite mailmen? Because they don't know who mailmen are. To an innocent puppy the outside world is a strange and threatening place. And, as my favorite American President once said: "We have nothing to fear, but fear itself." So it is imperative that you take responsibility for acquainting the new guy with his new world.

It is your obligation to assuage your puppy of his fears. How delightful it is to own a pup you can be proud of in the company of others. He should mature into an outgoing, happy, and enthusiastic fellow who greets everyone with cordiality and trust.

And how do you accomplish such a challenge? Simple. *Take him with you.* Take him in the car, in the boat, to the post office, to the fire department, to your relatives; to your friends...*take him with you.* Let him know and understand there are cats and other dogs in his world. There are babies and old geezers, buses and delivery people and all the other frightening things that he must contend with in *your* world.

But, here is the most important scheme in the proper socialization of your puppy. It is not enough just to introduce him to a new situation. It is imperative that this "new situation" be *harmless, joyful, and rewarding.* To insure that he comes to love and accept the mailperson, have the mailperson offer him a treat. Make sure when he meets his first cat, it is a happy and reassuring occasion. You should pet the cat and properly introduce the cat to your pup. Make a fuss over the pup to distract him from any suspicions he might have toward the cat.

Anticipate your pups first thunder storm and make sure that you are able to distract him from the threatening noise with fun and games and doggie treats.

And, do you know what? If you don't take the time and expend the energy to socialize your new puppy, you rightly deserve all of the future frustrations, exasperations, and infuriations that bad dog ownership entails.

Just as important as taking him out to the other world, is accustoming him to your world. Yes, you do have visitors. And, ordinarily, these visitors do not pose a threat. However, don't just take it for granted that your new puppy understands this. Take the high road when dealing with your new pet and anticipate how he might feel about intruders.

Have a friend(s) stop by at a given hour. Then as your friend approaches the house or apartment, talk to the dog in that goggley baby talk we mentioned earlier. You should point at the door or window in anticipation of a happy event. Ask your pup with exaggerated intonations: "Who's coming?" Create a display of happiness and excitement.

Exaggerate your greeting of your new friend(s) and insure that your friend(s) greeting of your puppy is equally enthusiastic. Making a favorable episode of newcomers will instill within the puppy's thinking that visitors are fun and not threatening to his wellbeing.

Don't worry about dissuading him of his watch-dog responsibilities. He will be just as excited about greeting a burglar as he is a friend.

English Shepherds are guard-dog neutral. They don't discriminate, greeting friend or foe with equal enthusiasm. But, then you don't have much choice with watch dogs. They either like everybody or bite everybody, so if you would prefer the latter type, get a Pit Bull.

English Shepherds are mostly lovers, not fighters. Although I remember as a child, my Dad used to torment old Shep by pretending he was wrestling with my mother. Of course, Dad had to gauge just how far his fooling could go because it wouldn't be long before old Shep would approach with his muzzle turn away, but still keeping an eye on the situation. Now, anyone who can read "dog" knows for sure that pose is a dog's warning signature. Muzzle turned away, but eyes clued on the subject means for sure that you had better back off or else.

I realize it is not customary to bring home two pups at the same time, but like the old song lyric that goes: "Two can't live as cheap as one, but I found out it's a lot more fun".

The adjustment to the new home is a whole lot easier for the pups if they can share their anxieties together. Also, I don't mean any offense, but to a pup you're not anywhere near as good looking as his litter mates. And besides, as far as he is concerned, his litter mates smelled a whole lot better than you do.

So if you have a very busy schedule, but still love the idea of having a pet about, get two pups so they can keep each other company while you are doing all that busy work you do.

One thing is for sure. You will be able to read and understand "dog" a whole lot easier once you compose a pack of two. It doesn't require a whole lot of observation to discern what they are talking about. Rather than more responsibility and effort, I have always found that, quite to the contrary, it is far easier and a lot more fun to have more than one dog about. For one thing, having two dogs absolves one of any guilt feelings on those days when you just don't want to be bothered with "dog". If one has a companion of his own sort, things will go swimmingly without you for the time being.

The single drawback to owning two pups is that you will have to separate them during training sessions. You will find it impossible to accomplish any sort of focus working one while the other is an observer.

And finally, you are going to find that training sessions become far less frustrating if you first let your dog(s) have a good run before commencing. Allowing him to run off some excess energy makes it much easier to compose and concentrate his focus on learning.

International Champion Snowy Rivers Sadie Lady CGC, HIC, NAC, NJC, NGC, N-T, OAC, OJC, O-T, V-OJC, V-OAC owned and trained by Connie Debusschere of Sweet Home, Oregon who is President of the United English Shepherd Association.

Your English Shepherd in Action

The English Shepherd, although classified as a herding dog, has always been a versatile fellow. Because of his high level of intelligence, his athleticism, his enthusiasm, his endurance and his easy trainability, Shep is a world class canine competitor.

Apart from just being your congenial pet, you might consider some organized fun events for both you and your pal. There are hosts of organizations that offer a chance to show off your prowess as a dog handler, and also really reap the far reaching rewards of English Shepherd ownership.

Boy oh boy! Should you decide to take up a team sport alongside of Shep, you couldn't make him any happier. That's what these guys live for. In his mind, working with his mistress or master is what life is all about.

Without question, joining with a group of truly nice people for fun and games will result in a guaranteed weight lose for you. This along with a sense of satisfaction and accomplishment you could otherwise never have imagined. And, in the meantime, you will make Shep the happiest, most grateful dog ever.

Shep is ready. Are You?

Following is a brief list of organized sports that offer canine competitions:

- Agility
- Rally Obedience
- Musical Canine Freestyle (Dancing with your dog)
- Flyball
- Herding

Although herding has historically been the English Shepherd's natural inclination, his higher calling, and inevitable mission in life, is to work alongside his mistress and perform whatever tasks are required of him. This genetic motivation, this zest to please has made these guys popular among active dog lovers for centuries.

Working together with your dog in an organized sport will not only demonstrate an example of complete intimate synergy, but also an expression of symbiotic closeness, and the true meaning of devotion.

Perhaps, because of the many popular television programs showing the agile abilities of dogs, this contest called **"Agility"** has become the sport we most associate with canine competitors.

Coming to the US from Great Britain in 1977, Agility is a fast paced sport in which a dog handler, with his dog off leash, is giving a set amount of time to course his dog through a variety of obstacles.

Patterned somewhat after show class horse events, Agility entails a series of jumps, teeter boards, weave poles, pause tables, "A" frames, pipe tunnels, and collapsed tunnels.

The obstacles are placed in different configurations usually uniquely different in each trial. Dogs are classified into different groups depending on their size and level of experience.

Most of the rules are fairly simple. The dog handlers may not touch either the equipment or their dogs while running the course.

They may; however, shout an unlimited number of commands or signals to the dog, and move freely anyway within the confines of the course perimeters.

The dogs will be faulted for not following the course precisely and in sequence. They will be penalized for knocking down a bar, failing to pause at the table, making contact with the "yellow zone" when ascending or descending the teeter boards or taking obstacles out of sequence. For each blunder, the dog will be accessed a time penalty deducted from the Standard Course Time. (SCT)

At the conclusion, the dog with the lowest number of faults and the fastest time wins his class or height division.

Following is a list of the largest agility organizations. Each also has a website and you can Google them for additional information:

United States Dog Agility Association (USDAA)
P.O. Box 850955, Richardson, TX 75085-0995

American Kennel Club (AKC)
5580 Center View Dr., Suite 200, Raleigh, NC 27606-3390

United Kennel Club (UKC)
100 East Kilgore Rd, Kalamazoo, MI 49001-5598

North American Dog Agility Council, Inc. (NADAC)
HCR 2, Box 277, St. Maries, ID 83861

Agility Association of Canada (AAC)
638 Wonderland Road South, London, ONT N6K 1L8

Agility is really a fun sport and one easy to take advantage of for the amateur.[13] Your dog is probably your biggest investment and the rewards are unlimited.

The equipment you might want to buy is readily available for you to set up a neat little course in your backyard.[14]

Herding competitions are my favorite. I have always been partial to the herding competitions mainly because I have trained a number of dogs to work with me over the years on the farm. I have never competed in herding competitions.

Each autumn I look forward to the "Scottish Games" in a nearby community. Not just for the thrill of listening to the majestic, bellicose splendor of the marching bagpipe bands resplendent in their august uniforms, not just for the tossing of the caber or the haggis, but for the enchantment of watching the shepherds work with their dogs.

What a joy that sight is for me. I have had a never ending fascination with the ability of the dogs to so closely communicate with their human counterparts.

The idea of a field trial is for the shepherd to control from three to six sheep by directing the activity of usually one or two herding dogs. Both time and discipline play an important role here for field judges will deduct points for each misstep of the dogs.

There are a variety of challenges set up for individual field trials, and usually the course and the time requirements are set in advance.

In most trials the dog(s) is required to handle a number of sheep that are some distance away. Basically, the dog must control the sheep and bring them to the handler.

Sometimes to complicate the dog's task, at some point in the field, they are required to drive the sheep away from the shepherd which is against every instinct of the dog. Therefore, an *away drive* is a real test of the dog's abilities.

The dog and handler working together should be able to move the sheep into a pen within an agreed time limit established before the trials begin.

Sometimes these trials require "shedding" which means the dog and handler must separate a bunch from the flock and pen them accordingly. A very difficult maneuver because sheep instinctively know there is safety in their numbers and will steadfastly refuse to be separated. This presents a real challenge to both the handler and the dog.

Many trails include a *cross drive* whereby the dog is directed to move the sheep in a straight line from one lateral perimeter of the field to the other some distance in front of the handler in a controlled, composed and unruffled manner.

One of the most difficult trials for a dog is called "singling" where he is required to single out one sheep from the group and move the animal in a controlled fashion away from the others.

Each of the requirements is assigned a predetermined score. For instance, the "cast" or " run out" may be counted as 20 points and the performance of each contestant will be awarded all or some portion of the total point score depending on the discretion of the judge.

Obviously I can't go too far into the training program of a herd dog here, but I would like to offer just a few insights that have helped me over the years and point you toward some excellent resources.

First off, if you go to the homepage of The United English Shepherd Association[15] there you will find a kick start to seek out some really good sources of information about herding dogs, and where to find similar organizations.

Another good source is the American Working Farm Collie Association[16] who feature the herding, guarding, and hunting aptitudes of the farm collies.

A really excellent source of stock dog information on the internet is called Stock Dog Server and these folks have done a terrific job of bringing together a complete and wide ranging catalog of information.[17]

Without a doubt the most unique and comprehensive resource for training your shepherd dog is: "E-Training for Dogs.Com.[18] At this site you can actually take a full length course in training your English Shepherd as a herding dog on the Web.

My first bit of advice I have for you when considering the training of your dog is to wait until she is old enough. I believe one of the biggest mistakes one can make with a herd dog is to start her too soon.

Until you pup has the legs and coordination to avoid being either confronted by or kicked by livestock, it is best to keep her leashed in their company.

It may seem a bit odd, but I like to first introduce my young scholars to chickens. Again, always on a lead, I casually walk these guys about the chicken yard always reassuring the pup to stay calm, and continually talk to the guy instructing her that no harm must come to these "wards" of ours.

Remember how I stressed the importance of the *sit, stay and come commands?* Well, don't even consider beginning herd training until your pup is proficient in the basics.

Secondly, I can't stress enough the importance of frequently reminding your dog to stay calm. Your pupil's ancestral past is certain to come to the fore when first introduced to livestock. You will immediately sense her rising excitement when she first comes in close contact with animals or poultry. That is why it is best to continue to leash the pup until she accustoms herself to being around livestock and remains relaxed.

Some old-timers begin their novices using ducks to herd. It seems to be a popular concept when starting young shepherd dogs. I have never tried this method. I think; however, in my experience, that geese may be a bit too much for the neophyte to cope with their orneriness.

Once you have confidence that your pup can restrain her natural desire to attack "prey", you can unleash her in the company of livestock.

Here is where her first test will come into play. It is called the "instinct test". She will immediately demonstrate either curiosity or fear.

If her instinctive reaction is obviously fear, it is time to immediately put her back on the leash for "confidence training".

Confidence training is simply a subtler means of introducing her to full size livestock. It requires that with patience and understanding you take a more gradual tact in reassuring her that no harm will come to her from the herd. Here it is important to remember not only patience, but to keep the succeeding sessions with livestock brief.

If, on the contrary, her reaction to first being introduced to livestock is curiosity, then always test her basic skills before unleashing her in the company of larger animals.

A brief review of her *sit, stay and come itinerary* will be in order before you allow her to continue unleashed.

If this is your first experience with herding, your training area is an important consideration. Although some prefer a large open pasture area, I much prefer closer confinement when starting a beginner. I simply feel that in a smaller area I will have more control of any unexpected circumstances that may arise.

Now it is time to allow you pup an opportunity for "controlled exploration". Let her advance toward the animals and observe her approach. Continue to speak to her softly using whatever terms come to mind. Here you must gage her level of excitement and continue to calm her with reassuring words of both encouragement and comfort. Easy, Easy, Easy. Good girl, good girl, etc.

Remain in control, recalling her frequently before she emerges into a state of excitement. Continue to bring her back to you so that she learns her basic focus must be on you, and that she is not allowed to freelance with the livestock.

What you will find, if you carefully observe her action and reaction, is that nature is already playing a major role in her learning curve. If, again, you continue to remind her to fix her focus on you and your commands, your dog is already half way to completing her sophomore curriculum in Herding 101.

Here are two important reminders. Keep your initial session brief, and remember to keep her focused on you.

I don't have space here to complete your herding education, but I can recommend a couple of valuable books, along with the "E-training for dogs.com" website that I mentioned earlier.

You might also want to go to the Stockdog Trainers in North America[19] to see if there is a local trainer near you or if you live in the Northeast try Northeast Trainers on the Web.[20]

My favorite book is: "Training and Working Dogs" By Scott Lithgow. Here is a comprehensive approach to teaching your dog a very relaxed approach to working with livestock.

Another good book on the subject is: Herding Dogs: Progressive Training, by Vergil S. Holland and Wait Jagger. My only criticism of this work is that they do tend to favor the Border Collie in their approach to herd training. There is a distinct difference between the two breeds when it comes to herding livestock.

Both of these books, by the way, are available at Amazon.com.

Next we come to **Flyball**. Essentially Flyball is a race between two teams comprised of four dogs each racing side–by–side over a 51 foot long course interrupted by four hurdles.

In relay fashion, each dog must run down over the jumps then trigger a box releasing a tennis ball and return over the jumps. Then the next dog in sequence is released to run the course, but can't cross the start line until the previous dog has returned completing four hurdles and reaching the start–finish line.

The North American Flyball Association, Inc.[21] is the home base for the sport and governs a lot of the sport's activities.

A good reference book: Flyball Racing: The Dog Sport for Everyone by Lonnie Olson is a good place to start. It is a complete guide for beginners and considers all aspects for beginners.

If you are interested in getting started with this sport go to the "club locator" web page[22] and you may find local groups in a nearby city to help you get started.

Rally Obedience is a relatively new competition designed to allow dog and handler teams to navigate thru a numbered course with signs indicating different exercises to perform.

It is sanction by The American Kennel Club AKC, The United Kennel Club, UKC, and the Association of Pet Dog Trainers; APDT[23] You don't have to be a member of APDT to participate in one of their rallies, however, your dog must be registered at the rally.

It should be noted here that English Shepherds are also eligible to compete in Obedience Trials sanctioned by the Australian Shepherd Club of American, ASCA[24]

English Shepherds are eligible to compete in UKC obedience trials testing the training of dogs as they perform a series of exercises at the command of their handler. [25]The levels of competition range from the basic "sit", "come" and "heel" to scent discrimination and directed retrieves over jumps.

In divided classes according to the experience of the handler, all dogs start with a perfect score of 200, and from there points are deducted in accordance with the performance of the handler and the dog.

Rally obedience is an opportunity to form a special bond with your dog unequaled in other sporting dog events.

At the Association of Pet Dog Trainer rallies all dogs, purebred, mixed breeds and dogs with disabilities are encouraged to enter. They offer three different levels of competition and a handler/dog team earns a Rally Title after successfully completing three course runs with qualifying scores.

Teams can also earn Championship titles, National Ranking awards and a special Award of Excellence.

Contestants can earn titles at each of three levels: Rally Novice (RN), Rally Advanced (RA) and Rally Excellent (RE).

Usually a judge will set up the course rally which consists of between 10 and 20 signs. With the dog at the handler's left side, at each numbered sign they will perform the indicated exercise, and then move to the next sign.

The handler may offer unlimited communication with her dog. At most rallies, the handler may not touch the dog or make physical corrections. Further, loud, or harsh signals or intimidating commands will be penalized.

The judge will watch for a smooth, even performance as well as the focus and skill demonstrated at each station. Rally obedience truly demonstrates the joys and fun of bonding with your pet."

Musical Canine Freestyle is "a choreographed musical program performed by handlers and their dogs. The object of musical freestyle is to display the dog and handler in a creative, innovative, and original dance, using music and intricate movements to showcase teamwork, artistry, costuming, athleticism, and style in interpreting the theme of the music. Heelwork–to–Music incorporates traditional dog obedience and the art of dressage with the inclusion of musical interpretation, dance elements, and costuming with an emphasis on the non–standard obedience movements. Both Musical Freestyle and Heelwork–to–Music routines should create a visually exciting display which is enjoyable to watch and which is equally enjoyable to dogs and handlers executing the programs."[26]

Along with the World Canine Free Style Association, there is also the Musical Dog Sport Association[27], and The Canine Freestyle Federation, Inc.[28]

Classes and membership applications are listed on each group's individual website. I have seen these programs on television from time to time, but I am a little curious about just why there seems to be a lack of participation by men?

I have often thought that the English Shepherd would make a most valuable **Therapy Dog**, principally because of his loving and outgoing nature.

There are numerous sites on the Internet for those who may be interested in making the rounds of hospitals–particularly children's wards—nursing homes, senior centers, schools, and special needs facilities. I have read so many good things about the benefits of therapy dogs, and how welcome their visits become to so many of those confined.

While exploring this subject on the web, I discovered that perhaps the easiest means of getting involved with therapy dog groups is to register with The Bright & Beautiful Therapy Dogs, Inc.[29]

Although there are others, it seems to me that this group, according to their website, makes it fairly easy to get started with therapy dog activities.

They are a nonprofit organization who will evaluate, test, train, qualify and assist therapy dog/handler teams in an effort to get them started toward a mission of goodwill where emotional service dogs are doing such a great job of providing for those in need.

I would think that for those less inclined toward participating in a sport type of activity, the idea of teaming up with your dog to spread happiness among those less fortunate would be one terrific idea.

Whatever you decide for you and your dog, ever if you forego an organized activity, remember that English Shepherds are active, enthusiastic dogs who enjoy not only a good romp, but one in concert with their beloved owner.

Your Dog's Nutrition

There are several myths we must first explore and dispel before we go into the fundamentals of feeding your pup.

Once upon a time, when I was a Public Relations Associate in The Big Apple; and worked for a very large conglomerate who owned, among a lot of other companies, one who produced and marketed a canned dog food product.

So, one might say I had the inside track on what goes on behind the scenes. One day I happened by the office of one of many veterinarians employed by this conglomerate. While we were chatting, I casually ask how it was possible to maintain the quality control of the different dog foods—one for pups, one for active dogs and one for senior dogs? I was shocked to learn, as he casually replied with a knowing smile: "We don't. We just print different labels."

I must admit I was skeptical of his response until one day I was visiting the production facility of the dog food plant. Low and behold there it was. Three labels all running out of one huge vat.

The recipe for dog food is referred to by the industry as the "computer mix". Each day or so their computer will look into the data base of feed prices, and search for the lowest prices for a suitable "mix". The data base contains a large selection of feed products and the available prices for the day. And, surprise, surprise the computer is programmed to select the cheapest products for the day to make up an appropriate mix.

The "mix" is going to contain a lot of corn and corn gluten meal, soybean meal, meat and bone meal along with wheat middlings and animal fat. There may be some mineral and vitamin additives also.

It is what we sometimes callously referred to in the trade as "corn and slaughter house floor- sweepings".

The more expensive mixes are going to contain: Lamb, brewer's rice, oatmeal, fishmeal and possible "poultry and by-products". Sometimes the computer will find dried egg products or non-fat dairy products if there is an oversupply on the market which subsequently means lowering the prices.

The moral of the story is never look on the front of the dog food bag to decide which brand you want to buy for your dog. Those glossy pictures of prime cuts of beef, chicken, and vegetables are just a slick come-on compared to what is actually inside of the bag. Consider a more realistic view. Sometimes you must even think of hide scraps and feathers as a "protein additive".

Always consult the side of the bag where the "guaranteed analysis" is printed and there you will find the percentage of "crude Protein". You will soon discover that the higher the "crude" protein content, the more expensive the brand is going to cost.

For example, a bag of whole corn at the feed store is going to contain about eight percent protein and cost about 16 to 20 cents a pound. Some dog foods contain as much as 27 percent protein. Therefore; creating a bag of mix starting with the most popular filler corn, at eight percent protein, and bringing the content mix up to 27 percent is going to cost the producer a great deal more than say a mix containing only 18 percent of protein.

And thus; any Animal Husbandry major who has studied the old stand-by: "Morrison's Feeds and Feeding" will be able to tell you that protein is needed for growth and sustenance, and that corn is needed to make your dog fat. So, it goes without saying, choose your dog's food accordingly.

The second myth we must dispel is that silly nonsense about not feeding your dog table scraps.[30] For example, my dear old deceased dad who was born at the end of the 19th Century had a lot of experience with farm dogs. One day I happened to ask him: "When you were a boy there were no dog food companies, so what did you feed your dogs?"

Believe it or not, he answered: "Just corn meal and some table scraps".

Gosh! Just think of that. Over a hundred years later—if we read the dog food labels–we are still feeding our dogs "corn meal and table scraps"...or slaughter house scraps as the case may be. I hate to be completely cynical about the marketing myth of dog foods, but doesn't it sometimes make you want to question: "Complete and balance formula"?

However, if we understand that Purina, Eukanuba, Iams and all the rest of the major dog food companies have a very large vested interest in Cornell, Tufts, Penn State, Texas A&M, UConn, etc., it is easy to understand why young veterinary students might be predisposed to tout the evils of table scraps. And, in turn, persuade and encourage you to follow strictly a commercial dog food diet for your dog.

I can only conclude that after a hundred years or more of rising, breeding, and training dogs, we Hammond's have been supplementing our dog foods with table scraps, and we have never lost a single dog to malnutrition.

Dog foods, just like human foods and other pet foods, are regulated under the Federal Food, Drug, and Cosmetic Act. Also like all foods marketed in this country, they must be truthfully labeled and contain ingredients that are (GRAS) which stands for *generally* reco*gniz*ed *as Safe*. Interestingly, as long as they are GRAS, *they do not require* FDA approval before they are marketed.

There is one other assurance on the dog food label you can look for: AAFCO which stands for: The association of American Feed Control Officials. This seal is supposed to mean that the dog food meets the basic requirements for providing complete and balanced nutrition for dogs.

Now, I am sure that we all know that labeled ingredients of pet foods, just like human foods, are required to be listed in descending order by weight. However, moisture in the ingredients makes it a bit complicated to interpret. For instance: chicken which can be up to 65-70 percent water may be listed ahead of dry ingredients like corn meal, soybean meal or wheat middlings which may be only 10 percent water.

In this case, chicken may be listed as the first ingredient over the corn, soybean, and wheat causing you to believe that chicken is the predominant ingredient. While in fact; the three meal and middlings, when added together may indeed outweigh the chicken ingredients.

Another ruse to confuse in labeling involves lumping. For example, let's say the first four ingredients read: poultry products, rice, whole grain corn, corn gluten meal, etc. The last two are both forms of corn so if they were lumped together instead of listed separately they would move up the list and perhaps even dominate the recipe.

You should very quickly conclude that all isn't what it appears to be on labels and those corporate giants out there competing for your dog-food dollar can be very tricky devils. *Sometimes they are even deceptive.*

There are a number of extreme diets available. Although *I* would not strictly endorse them, I think you should know about and consider them for your dog.

BARF or *Biologically Appropriate Raw Food*[1], and sometimes referred to as just *Bones and Raw Food,* is just what it purports to be. It is a complete and inclusive regimen of raw foods that are primarily made up of raw chicken, chicken parts, beef, organ meats, etc. Admittedly, I have never tried this approach to feeding my dogs; however, *I don't believe it is extreme by any means.*

I have this theory that nature knows best. Whenever I become puzzled about a question regarding my dogs, I ask myself simply: What would nature provide or what would nature do?

Frankly, I cannot disagree with those who believe in this BARF diet for dogs. However, when it comes to feeding raw chicken, I become "chicken".

Such a practice is scary to me because I have had to, on a couple of occasions, reach down a dog's throat to retrieve a bone lodged there. Now the proponents of this diet claim that raw bones do not shatter, and therefore will not lodge. Again, I remain more than a little leery or "chicken" about feeding *raw* chicken.

Secondly, I have too many dogs to afford such a practice. With eight or ten English Shepherds to feed twice a day, I think the cost might outweigh the benefits in my case. But again, I make no attempt to dispute this theory of nutrition for dogs. To be just, I have not investigated the idea completely only because of the two reasons I have just stated. But, if you are so inclined, I encourage you to look into the matter.

In opposition to the BARF diet, I suppose one might consider the vegetarian or vegan diet for one's dog.[32] There are, of course, several variations on the vegetarian diet. Some vegetarians allow for eggs and dairy products, while others strictly rely on vegetables only to the total exclusion of all animal products. (Herbivore)

If we consider humans as omnivores, or those who eat both plants and meat, than only to a lesser extent are we able to liken our dogs to similar taste. It must be understood that in the wild, the dog (scientific order carnivore, meat eater.) upon making a kill will normally first devour the intestines of his prey. Because his prey is considered an herbivore, the intestine will provide the canine with plant nutrition; and the remaining carcass satisfies his need for high protein meat.

A dog's nutritional requirements, such as the need for relatively high amounts of protein and calcium, reflect the dietary limitations of plant foods as a total diet. I confess that I have never explored the possibility of a vegetarian diet.

It is obvious that a dog's teeth are designed for eating a diet largely comprised of animal tissue. The dog's short intestinal tracts compared to humans, and especially to animals like sheep or cows, also indicate they are not designed to accommodate diets containing large amounts of plant materials.

(Again, a good reason for supplementing commercial dog foods comprised mostly of corn with meaty table scraps from your table.)

If you have a concern for reducing the intake of saturated fats and cholesterol by cutting meats out of the diet, such concern would not be of any real health benefit, except possible in the case of senior dogs, because both dogs and cats do not suffer from problems such as high cholesterol or coronary artery disease nearly as much as humans.

I am not a nutritionist; so therefore, before I would pass judgment on any of these radical diets I think the solution may be a whole lot more simple than we suppose.

I suggest if you aren't a mother, than ask your mother what to feed your dog. Mom's has been providing a "balanced ration" for children and families for years.

And, dogs have been a large part of families for thousands of years–certainly long before professional nutritionist and veterinarians. I don't think your dog's menu should be any more complicated than mom's menu for the whole family. Don't let "the professionals" scare you. Having been a "Corporate Player" for years, I know it is reasonable to advise you that given the choice–trust Mom.

Here's something else to think about when those "professionals" warn us that only they have the "inside track" and are solely capable of deciding what to feed your dog.

Considering the many dog food recalls in recent years, along with other foul up's by dog food manufacturer. Perhaps it is more than fair to speculate that those who claim to have the "inside track" on canine nutrition had better watch where they step on that track.

Now, some might ask about dietary supplements for their dogs. Ordinarily I would say no to any supplement not approved by your dog's doctor. I once ask my veterinarian about people vitamins for my dogs and her response was simply: "Wouldn't hurt". Of course, because vitamins are mostly fat and water soluble, I guess it follows that she meant regardless of whether they help or not they are harmless.

I know how difficult it is for you to accept the premise that your English Shepherd puppy is not a little person with a fur coat. Despite how much a part of your family he has become, he really isn't people. For that reason you should be very cautious about feeding unapproved feeds and feed supplements to your pet just because of advertising claims.

For instance, Pfizer Pharmaceuticals has recently come out with a diet pill for dogs; which by the way, has been approved by the FDA. How absolutely silly. I have a counter suggestion–take your dog for a walk.

Perhaps you have seen advertisements for glucosamine and chondroitin which claim to limit joint pain. Nonsense.

You may have also seen claims for St. John's Wort, supposedly to treat doggy depression. Unlike Pfizer's product, these have not been approved, and their claims are pure bunkum.

The same consideration given to animal food supplements by the FDA applies also to food additives. As such, they are not permitted in pet food.

You must be realistic when it comes to putting your faith in dog food labels. Just as some wealthy public figures get away with murder, you must understand that neither the FDA nor State authorities have nearly enough employees in their numbers to monitor every food manufacturer or pet supplier.

Preventing those unscrupulous profiteers who use unapproved ingredients from selling their products is just impossible. *This same limitation of enforcement personnel also applies to those who will misrepresent percentage of crude protein.* The profit motive here far outweighs the risk of being caught. That is why it is imperative for you to first check with your vet *before offering any supplement* to your pet.

Would you believe there are several beef flavored doggie beers on the market today including Happy Tail Ale? Are we not going a bit too far with this nonsense of adding to and supplementing our pet's diet?

One of the unsung characteristics of the English Shepherd dog is that special quality of being "thrifty" by nature. Old timers referred to this feature as being "good on gas". Thrifty meaning you can get a lot of mileage out of your shepherd for relatively little food. A bowl of kibbles goes a long way with English Shepherds that are capable of running for hours. Bear this in mind when portioning out your shepherd's daily fare.

Oddly enough, the American Obesity Association reports that 64.5 percent of Americans are overweight and 30.5 percent are obese. Can it be a coincidence these are almost the same reported statistics concerning dogs and cats entering US pet clinics?

When it comes to feeding our dogs, we should be aware that pet-food makers are laying a big fat guilt trip on us. More than a hundred million dollars is spent each year, almost 80 percent on TV, to tell us we should "feed" our dogs a little more love. In fact, Purina notes: "All you add is love".

Before we discuss what to feed, let's first talk about what *not* to feed. Number one, and at the very top of your list, should be *NOT TOO MUCH.*

An overweight pet is not a happy pet. There are many instances of owners feeding their dogs to the point whereby the poor fat beast finds proper self-grooming very difficult. So fat, in fact, unable to reach around to groom his hind sides.

Common sense tells us that dogs, like many of us, haven't much discipline when it comes to controlling food intake. At this point I must tell you that my English Shepherd dogs, who have access to their large yard, keep themselves fit and trim. I believe it is their inherent happy, active nature that keeps them healthy, and vibrant. Of course, I make an effort not to overfeed.

Please notice, in the above comment; I mentioned "my dogs". Here again, there is an advantage to owning dogs in their plurality. If you are being completely honest with yourself, you know full well that you are not going to be able to offer your dog daily exercise on a routine bases. Here is where multiple dog ownership has a real advantage for you. Basically, you won't have to feel guilty about ignoring your poor, sad-eyed pup on those days when you absolutely can't take him for his daily jaunt.

However, if he has a buddy living with him, there is little doubt you will be forgiven for your lapses. Together, they will run off any of those excess' you feed them...within reason.

Do not feed your dog chocolate which contains both caffeine and theobromine. Simply put, a dog's digestion can't deal with these substances and in some cases it can prove fatal. Although, dark chocolate is far more toxic to your dog than white chocolate, neither is acceptable in their diet.

Also on the no-no list are: Onions, grapes, raisins, and fresh garlic.

Another no-no is an excess of rich fatty foods. Most every Thanksgiving veterinarians see a lot of patients suffer from Pancreatites. A crisis brought on as a result of eating too much turkey, dressing, and all the fixings. The pancreas cannot cope with the overload. The consequences are depression, lethargy; vomiting, diarrhea and fever along with severe abdominal pain. Avoid Pancreatites by avoiding rich, fatty foods in excess.

Super bowl Sunday is another of those dangerous "holidays" for dogs. Gee, isn't it fun to share your beer with your dog when the party gets going? Shep is a riot when you get a few beers in him. Because alcohol toxicity can be fatal to dogs, it is best not to share your celebratory inebriation with him.

There is an infinite variety of diets that are fed. Some might include:

Canned food
Kibble with canned
Kibble only
Kibble with flavor toppers
Kibble with vegetables
Other real food
Raw food (BARF)
Home cooked diet
Prescription diets

After some experimentation, I have discovered my Shepherds prefer a varied regime. I find they tend to lose interest in their food dish if the diet becomes routine and too monotonous. Instead of chowing down right away, their feed dishes sometimes remain half full for a good part of the day. At least until they become convinced that they will have to take it, or leave it.

Because of the cost, I have found that canned food is not practical for the English Shepherd as a one course feeding. Most canned dog foods are from 70 to 80 percent moisture (water). It can become very expensive to consider canned dog food as a singular diet for a medium size dog like the English Shepherd.

You can decide if your choice of diet is correct by simply observing your dog's coat. A dog's fur is the first indicator of the animal's health and conditioning.

All English Shepherds have a medium length coat which can be straight, wavy, or curly with a healthy dense undercoat. The coat should have a bright, soft shinning surface that appears lush and dense.

The second health indicator is a bright, alert, and perky eye in combination with nicely colored pink gums. That is to say that a bright eyed and bushy tailed dog assuredly enjoys a healthy diet and is fit.

In many cases it is possible to deal with health problems by consulting with your veterinarian about diet. Many allergies are directly related to diet. Other problems such as arthritis, kidney failure, cardiac conditions, and liver disease can be helped with a specialized diet.

Be sure when you visit your veterinary clinic that you take along some notes about your dog's appetite and menu including some idea about her drinking water intake.

You can be sure that pet food products will follow the trends in human food. Low-fat, low-carb, all-organic, sodium free, whatever is current because pet manufacturers know how closely you identify with your dog. It is a given that dog lovers are considerably more anthropocentric than normal people.

However, you must give yourself credit. It follows that if you are smart enough to choose one of the most intelligent dog breeds, you are fully competent to choose his meal menus.

That's right. If you have an English Shepherd pal at home, there is no question that you do not follow the pack. You did not pick out a novelty dog or popular breed pup. You have already demonstrated that you can think for yourself. That means you are adept at looking after yourself and others.

Because my dogs are family, I enjoy dreaming up new recipes and introducing new items to their diet.

One of my favorites is Totally Chicken. If you have a pressure cooker it is easy to prepare several meals ahead that will last for a few days. I wait until I can find a good deal on chicken at the supermarket. Ideally, if you can buy chicken for 49 to 89 cents a pound—compare this price to the *unit price* of premium dog food—and you know you have a deal.

Follow the instructions that came with your pressure cooker. Just add chicken, salt, spices and other veggies. The idea is to cook the chicken whole...bones and all. Except, instead of cooking just for the prescribed amount of time, continue cooking three or four times longer or until you have broken down the bones completely.

Actually, you are going to feed the whole chicken because at this stage the bones are no longer brittle. Just think about how much natural bone calcium you're adding to your dog's diet. That's how the dog food manufacturers do it. Believe me they do not debone.

I use the chicken along with the broth to pour over kibble rounding out a tasty, nutritious meal for my guys. You can improvise. It's possible to cool the cooker completely, and then add some rice or noodles if you prefer. Then just follow your pressure cooker's recipe book for the cooking time for the remainder.[33] Also on the cheap, think about adding dried peas or beans to the mix.

I have also found that I can make my own dog biscuits in my bread machine.[34] Again, a quick and easy treat for your guys at half the cost of milk bones. And here again, you can be absolutely sure of the nutritional value of your home cooking.

Another of my basic English Shepherd recipes is gruel. Remember earlier how I remarked that protein will make you grow, and corn will make you fat? I like oats in my dog's diet. If I could look into their past, I am certain in their ancestral home in the British Isles these dogs routinely enjoyed a bit of gruel with their masters daily. I also think that oatmeal can solve those occasional bowel movement problems your dog may suffer.

Because most dog kibble is mainly corn, I like to mollify the kibble with some oat mixture. You know how easy it is to stir up a bowl of oat meal. Quick and easy to do, however, I like to add to the boiling water a couple of beef or chicken bouillon cubes before adding the cereal. I also like to add a dollop of molasses (iron and trace minerals) or a squirt of maple syrup as a taste enhancer. My dogs truly relish this recipe for oat meal.

Sometimes I am able to find eggs on sales for as little as eight cents apiece. Wow! Think of all that good protein for your guy, and mixed with a little pasta or oatmeal, a whole lot cheaper than commercial dog food.

With a little imagination and some really inexpensive ingredients, there are unlimited resources for providing your English Shepherd a home cooked meal at least a few times every week.[35]

At this point, are you mumbling something to yourself about who has time to cook for the dog(s)? If that be the case, it is blatantly obvious that you have two major problems.

First of all, you are assuredly not stopping. Secondly, you sure as heck are not smelling any roses either.

Take a break. Slow down. Get to know your family and your dog(s). Your dog is a whole lot more interesting, and a whole lot less taxing than your personal rat race anyway.

Why fuss for your dog and make certain of proper nutrition? Because you know in your heart of hearts, deep within your anthracitic being there is *only one* who offers you total devotion. Not that two- faced neighbor bitch, not those ungrateful offspring who never call, not that inattentive spouse, nor that ungrateful, churlish boss.

There is but one devoted suitor in your life who is so completely dedicated to you—is absolutely consumed by a need to please and attend to only you. You can search the world over, but there is only one true lover in your life–and your absolute best friend.

And...it goes without saying...

Health Care

The English Shepherd is a pretty hearty breed. I have owned and bred these dogs for years going back over a half a century.

Apart from the routine maintenance of having their shots; and an occasional vet check before and after birthing, there is little to be said for either congenital or developmentally assimilated health problems.

I know there is some history of hip dysphasia among all medium to large size dogs, but I have never encounter the problem with an English Shepherd. However, that is not to say that it doesn't exist. Maybe it is just my luck.

That said; let's begin with considering the best environment for your English Shepherd. Outside–Alfresco–fuera–dehors–im freien.

I have never understood the idea of keeping a dog in the house for extended periods. Of course, there is a mutual sense of fellowship being with your dog. However; it goes without saying that God didn't build housing for his creatures.

So if you want a healthy, happy dog why not try nature's way. Except for extremely hot days, your dog should be outside as much as possible. Notice I said "hot" days. English Shepherds withstand the cold much more so than they do the heat.

It is also a given that your dog's nose is hundreds of times more sensitive that yours. Think for a moment about all of those concentrated and extraneous odors inside your home—household cleaners, toiletries, artificial fibers, etc.

Give the poor guy a break. There are enough foreign and exotic odors in your home to make him decide he would rather be outside with Thumper and that bashful polecat Flower.

I once had the privilege of knowing Dr. James Brennen, who was a dear friend of James Herriot...the English writer/veterinarian of "All Creature Great and Small" fame.

One day upon meeting Dr. Brennen, I remarked that some of my cows had contracted ring worm. Dr. Brennen inquired if the cows were in the barn. I answered in the affirmative because it was wintertime.

"Turn 'em out"! He stated firmly. "All critters welcome the Lord's elements both fair and foul. Good for both their constitution and immunity."

I turned out the cows for the reminder of the winter, except for extreme bad weather conditions, noting they soon became a happier, healthier lot, and, the ring worm disappeared without any need of treatment.

Since that day I have been a firm believer in the great outdoors for all my dogs and other critters.

Not to beat a dead horse, but it has to be distressing for your pet if she hasn't been acclimated from fall unto winter.

Being outside a good part of the time during the soft breezes of autumn conditions her to accept the hash winds of winter.

Just as you add layers of clothing as the autumnal climate chills, so must you allow nature to adjust the density of your dog's coat for when the frosty weather bites?

Before we get into the nitty gritty of dog care there are a couple of things to consider while we are on the subject of nature.

As I have said before, I have enjoyed good healthy, hearty English Shepherd dogs for years. I sometimes attribute this to a practice of prevention. Yogurt, molasses, fish oil, and brewer's yeast have been my old standby for years. I am not sure if this helps, but I'm afraid to quit what appears to be working for me now.

I particularly like yogurt for my bitches during their gestation periods, and as well, for their pups after whelping. I believe it contributes greatly to building and boosting their immune system. (And, parenthetically, if you have ever seen a dog drag (scoot) his behind across the floor, a good dose of yogurt in his food will in most cases remedy that problem.)

I like molasses for its iron and trace mineral content, and I believe the fish oil and brewer's yeast inhibit ticks and fleas along with being a very good circulation and heart tonic. I think the fish oil also contributes to a really nice coat.

After my bitches wean their pups and blow their coats, I add lots of fish and fish oil to their diets.

Along with adding fish to their diet regularly, I also feed Omega 3 fish oil tablets to my guy's regime.

Now let's talk about canine vaccines. They are essential for the health of your dog. It would be cheaper if you sent off for the serums and actually did the vaccines yourself—much cheaper in fact.

However, this whole business of the potential for canine disease should be left in the hands of a profession. You really should discuss–and I do mean hold a discussion–with your veterinarian about an appropriate schedule of vaccines for your pet.

In order to prepare you for such a discussion, let's go over briefly a tour of the common potential diseases.

I believe that every State now has some mandate for vaccinating all dogs against **Rabies**. There is no cure for this virulent and dreadfully agonizing death which soon follows the infection. Pups usually get a temporary vaccine, following by revaccination at one year of age. And, then every three years depending on State laws.

Canine Distemper a severe multi-systemic virus is endemic of coming in contact with bodily secretions of infected animals. Symptoms are cold-like nasal discharge, red eyes followed by vomiting, diarrhea, fever, and possibly convulsions. Again, a pup should have a temporary vaccine at six and ten weeks of age; and a revaccination at one year of age, and again every three years.

Heartworm is now a contagion in all 50 States and can be fatal. Actually infection stems from a mosquito bite. Maybe you have seen the poster in your Vet's office depicting the infected canine heart infested with thousands of long spaghetti-like worms.

Preventive doses come in oral and topical versions and are only available from a veterinarian. Diethylcarbamazine is given daily. Ivermectin (Heartguard,) Milbmycin (Interceptor) and Moxidectin (ProHeart) are given monthly. Selamectin (Revolution) is a new preventive applied topically. Some of these drugs also kill other parasitic worms. Revolution also acts against fleas, ticks, and mites.

Tick bites are the cause of **Lyme disease**, also known as borrelia burgdoferi. It is diagnosed by observing fever, lethargy, swelling in the bitten limb and depression. If treated within the first week of symptoms the dog will usually respond to an antibiotic regime that usually is administered for about three weeks. This is an optional vaccine you should discuss with your Vet; however, in high-risk areas I would recommend an annual injection.

Canine Parvovirus, sometimes mistaken for doggie flu is deadly with only a 50/50 chance of survival in older dogs and usually fatal in puppies. This virus can live for many months outside of its host. Vaccinate puppy, and then again at one year of age. Follow on then every three years.

A highly contagious upper respiratory infection, **Canine Adenovirus-2** shows symptoms of a dry, hacking cough. Prognosis is poor to good depending on the dog's age and condition. You should really talk this vaccine over with your vet who will advise you if there is a need for this procedure. Also protects against CAV-2, but again, this vaccine should be administered only upon your Vet's recommendation.

Parainfluenza Virus is a type of kennel cough that exhibits a nasal discharge along with a persistent cough which often also causes gagging. This condition should not be left untreated. There is a vaccine available.

There are two types of vaccines for you to consider when talking with your vet. **Core** vaccines prevent life-threatening disease while **non-core** vaccines describe less common diseases.

Ordinarily we would not question the practice of vaccinating our dogs. Of course, over the past fifty years much progress has been made in overcoming a canine's susceptibility to tragic and life threatening disease.

However, of late, there is growing evidence that over vaccinating our dogs can create a vulnerability to illnesses.

Actually, this means chronic conditions such as anemia, arthritis, gastrointestinal and thyroid disorders, cancer, seizures, and allergies.

There is even the risk of over stimulating the immune systems to the point whereby the dogs own tissue system begins to break down. The latter may manifest itself in blood, nervous system, thyroid, or skin diseases. These symptoms usually remain clandestine until months after the actual vaccination.

Perhaps instead of routine annual vaccinations, the alternative may be the "Titer Test". The Titer takes blood for an annual test to determine your dog's immune defenses. The tests are readily available, not terribly expensive and offer multiple advantages over the practice of either over vaccinating or under vaccinating as a mere routine procedure.

In summary, consult with your veterinarian before blindly submitting your pet to the needle.

I would be remiss if I were too continued before first helping you both select and evaluate the veterinarian who will be responsible for your dog's health and wellbeing. Why bother, you might well say?

Or perhaps, you already have a family vet who is both courteous and attentive.

Well, if you are currently satisfied with your dog's medical care please ignore the remainder of this page. But, from my point of view, *courteous and attentive* just don't cut it.

If you are seeking a vet for your new puppy, here are some considerations you might opt for: First of all, don't wait until an emergency occurs before finding a vet. That might be too late.

Secondly, don't ask friends to recommend someone. They will, as a matter of course, refer you to their vet who: "is a nice guy, friendly and courteous".

I think there are a few other people who might have a more authentic knowledge of a local vet's reputation. I would first ask dog trainers, groomers, pet sitters, animal shelter workers, or pet store clerks.

Some vets belong to the American Animal Hospital Association (AAHA) and are required to meet certain standards in the area of facilities, equipment, and quality care. This *might* be a factor in your selection.

Most important of all for you to consider is emergency services. How does this vet handle emergencies? Will she make house calls? What are her clinic's hours? Will you be referred to another hospital or clinic after-hours? Consider these possibilities should you need a vet in a life or death situation.

Next in importance, I believe, is can you talk to this guy and the members of her staff? Is there a potential for full and open communication here? Will she respect your views and concerns, or is she elite, inflexible, and dogmatic in her "chrome tableside manner?"

It goes without saying that you are going to expect the cleanliness and sanitary conditions to be impeccable, but you might ask about the available equipment on the premises. Things such as x-rays, ultrasound, blood work, EKG, endoscopes, etc. Are these procedures done in-house or referred to a specialist?

Don't become too concerned about the available equipment, or the office luxuries, because as a rule of thumb billing escalates in direct proportion to the amount of chrome in the workspace.

If a fellow has a quarter of a million invested in equipment and décor, he is going to be somewhat anxious to amortize his debt as soon as possible.

Another consideration, and although minor, is whether the vet is a general practitioner or one who just specializes in small animals.

I suppose over the years because I have lived in different parts of the country, I have used the services of at least a dozen or more vets. Generally speaking, I prefer the general practice vet.

Maybe I have arrived at this prejudice because I have *always* found them to be cheaper than the guys who do just dogs and cats. I suspect that, if a vet's previous house call was yanking on the tongue of a large mare while floating her teeth, than a simple subcutaneous injection into a dog's fur flap comes as somewhat of a relief.

And, because these vets work out of the back of their pick-ups or vans a good part of the day, their stationary clinic back home is somewhat more Spartan in décor and reflects a subtle sense of frugality.

It is important to know when your dog is sick to the point where she needs veterinary attention.

My English Shepherds will go off their feed from time to time and that is not unusual for them.

However, it is important to begin watching for any related conditions. Temporary loss of appetite is not a major concern unless it can be related to chronic diarrhea or excessive vomiting. If, for instance, you observe either of these symptoms then you must begin associating these conditions with other changes in behavior. Is the dog sleeping excessively, drinking large amounts of water, whining or displaying any changes in her social interactions?

If you have either a rectal or inter-ear thermometer a check of her body temperature will give you a meaningful reading of her physical condition. (A dog's normal body temperature is between 101.5 and 102.5 degrees Fahrenheit).

If you get any abnormal reading either above or below, it is time to consider making that phone call to the veterinary. Otherwise, if all else seems normal, than you may just want to restrict her food intake for 12 to 24 hours either totally, or feeding just small amounts of easily digestible chicken or rice.

This practice seems to settle the gastrointestinal system and may eliminate the problem. You can also try some anti-diarrheals such as kaopectate or pepto-bismol if bowel movements are the problem. Keep a sharp eye on the situation, and if the problem persists than it is time to make an appointment with your vet.

Incidentally, here is an example whereby you can avoid costly trips to the veterinary. If you are able to take your dog's temperature reading you can tell right off if there may be a problem.

If you can't or are unsure of taking temperatures, then the next time you are at the clinic ask the doc to show you how to take a temperature reading along with a demonstration. If he's any kind of guy, he will be more than happy to accommodate you. If he hesitates—change vets.

Allergies present a problem for some dogs, although I haven't found that to be the case with my English Shepherds. It is astounding to me that recent dog surveys have reveal that fully 20 percent of American dogs have been diagnosed with one form of hypersensitivity or another.

Of course, allergies cannot be cured, but there have been recent advances in control to make them tolerable for your dog to live with.

In the case of the English Shepherd I believe one major factor plays an important role in their ability to be somewhat free of allergies.

In their favor, this dog has never been bred for the show ring. Therein, I firmly believe, lays the key to their superior immunity. There has never been any restriction placed on the breeder to make them: bigger or smaller; wider–narrower; more–less colorful;–higher–lower, etc.

The dogs have been bred to simply follow explicit directions in the meadow, standby friends, and family, and love everybody–especially children.

The surprising little secret in establishing a universal standard to which all "show dogs" must conform is a hushed subject. Those who breed "pretty dogs" rarely talk much about how they succeed in conforming to the "Standard".

How does one meet the mandated "Standard" in all succeeding generations? How does one conform to "the norm"?

In a phrase: Incest is best. In fact, without some degree of inbreeding there would be no perfect show dogs.

So far English Shepherd breeders have avoided prettying-up their dogs for the show ring.

Now: the Agility course or the herding competitions–where you have to do more than just look pretty–where brains count more than beauty–that's where English Shepherds shine.

Dental care is a sometimes an issue with the English Shepherd as is the case with all dogs.

Actually, there is more of a dental problem with toy breeds and smaller dogs. I know I should routinely brush my dog's teeth, but that is usually one of the last things on my list when it comes to kennel chores.

Most times I rationalize my failing here by purchasing a number of heavy shin and shank bones at the meat department. My dogs will gnaw on those things for hours.

Firmly, I believe this is the reason for not having dental problems with my dogs.

Don't discard those big shank bones when they have all the meat scraps and marrow gone. Take a spoon and fill them with peanut butter, really stuffing the goop way done into the cavity. You dog will lick and gnaw some more and you will can get additional usage out of them while adding a lot of protein to their diet.

Despite marketing claims, commercial dog bones and biscuits are of little use and of no value when it comes to dental care. They do, however, serve as a source of added nutrition for your dog.

Your vet may have available either chlorhexidine spray or mouthwash, but these products are not as effective as actually brushing your dog's teeth.

When you brush your dog's teeth, use a child's toothbrush with some diluted baking soda. Concentrate your movements on that area where the gum margin meets with the crown of the tooth. That is where most tartar buildup begins.

Briefly we can deal with doggy halitosis, but if it is severe, it is a job for your veterinary. Tatar is the buildup of a combination of bacteria, mineral and decomposed food. No wonder it stinks.

Sometimes pups when shedding their baby teeth tend to drool a lot while exhibiting bad breath. In this case, the only solution is to brush for baby.

Bad breath in older dogs may be caused by excessive tartar buildup which in most cases has to be removed by the vet. Don't ignore bad breath in older dogs because in some cases it may be indicative of either kidney or liver disease. It can be harmful to ignore this symptom in older dogs and you should mention it to your vet on your next visit.

Older dogs can become somewhat of a problem, and for them to age gracefully requires special care. Most important for senior dog health and longevity is, once again, your need to maintain proper weight throughout your dog's lifetime.

You know a dog is in good condition when he shows just a trace of rib. Note I said *trace*. If you can't feel your dog's ribs or, detect a waistline, then more than likely you dog is overweight.

In order to determine your dog's age you have to do a little math. And, I don't mean that old myth about one human year equals seven dog years. In some cases that would mean teeny bopper bitches would be whelping pups.

No, we have to be a bit more realistic. How about the first two years of your dog's life we count individually as 9 to 12 years each on the human scale of one year? Meaning that at human age two; your dog is somewhere between 18 and 24 years old. That's about right because this is when the bitches mature and begin to bear pups. Thereafter; we add doggy years at a rate of four doggy years to each human one.

If you do the math, that would put your dog in the senior citizen class at about age 12. Here, remember we are talking exclusively about the English Shepherd breed or a medium size dog. Allowances will have to be made for larger breeds. I have owned St. Bernard's and Great Danes that were ready for Social Security at eight or nine years of age.

As a general rule, you can expect your English Shepherd to live to about 14 years of age. That is about the life expectancy of the breed.

Not a lot of research has gone into the lifespan of the breed; however, if we look at their cousins the Border collie and the Australian Shepherd we are in the ball park here. Most of my dogs live well past their 14- year peak; some have still been around at age 19.

Do we have to pause here and mention *diet* and *exercise*?

It may be alright to skimp on vet examines when your dog is young, but as he grows older it becomes more essential that he have regular checkups.

Hey, this guy has given you a lot of good years. Years of loyalty and friendship, and it is during these September years that you are going to have to spring for at least an annual checkup for the elderly guy. Preferably, semi-annual would be better if you can afford it.

As the years pass for your English Shepherd his surroundings will begin to dim. Cataracts, glaucoma, and retinal atrophy are things to look for as your old pal ages. Watch to see if there is any filming or color changes in his eyes. Observe the way he walks, if he hesitates, to determine if he is having difficulty with his vision.

Is he having difficulty hearing you? Hearing loss can lead to stress indicated by a change in behavior. Is he barking excessively or does he appear confused?

And speaking of being confused, dogs also experience Alzheimer's disease as they progress in age just like humans. It is a cognitive dysfunction indicative of temporary disorientation and sometimes aggressive reactions to quite normal situations.

Oddly enough, my older guys haven't become anywhere's near as cranky as I have become in my old age.

Along with kidney and liver function, there is also heart, prostate and hypothyroidism to deal with as your old friend enters the winter of his years. This is not the time to neglect exercise. Even if she hesitates, you must coax her a bit to walk and get the blood circulating every day. This will be less of a problem to deal with if you maintain her proper weight. Consult with your vet about a diet for her. Some say that these older less active dogs don't require as much protein as their younger counterparts.

But, eventually you are going to have to say good-by to her. Euthanasia is always a difficult decision. A conclusion that for days and sometimes weeks will pull at your heartstrings. Of course; having a two-dog family always makes this resolution a bit easier, but even then, you hope against hope that you can hang on to your old buddy just a bit longer.

It has been my sad duty on a number of occasions to have to euthanize an old friend. If it be any consolation for you, it is a very gentle and quiet way to end a life. After the infusion of a controlled sedative, she gradually closes her eyes and goes placidly off to sleep. You should consider euthanasia your final act of love for your old and faithful pal.

Who is Your English Shepherd?

More than likely, like most pet lovers, you may be suffering from a very misleading concept of just who your dog is really. All too often we have this mythical concept of perceiving all dogs as being just like the movie version of "Lassie".

The Lassie stereotype is a very "warm puppy concept" and very comforting. However; you will get along much better with your dog, and have a much better chance of training her, if you take a different tact all together. Success demands that you change your notion about who your English Shepherd *really* is.

You must first understand that your dog is not estranged from you in that she considers herself a different being or life form. In your dog's eyes, you and your family are just larger versions of herself. Together you, your family, and your dog(s) are just one big loving pack all living together in one cozy den.

And, before you begin to challenge this premise, it is only fitting for you to keep in mind this hypothesis is a *"good thing"*.

A dog requires a social order that mandates her limits and social parameters. Without these mandated social limits, and without exception, your dog will soon become neurotic and possible even psychotic. There will be times when you will have to become very stern with your pet. It will be natural for you to hesitate because you may feel guilty about compelling her to obey, or remorseful about your reprimands when her behavior becomes unacceptable.

Remember the old maxim: "this is going to hurt me more than it will hurt you"? More than likely it will, but bear in mind that unless your dog receives proper and disciplined guidance from you, she will soon become a Freudian canine misfit.

Except for the Alpha dog, all the rest are followers and you do them a disservice if you don't provide very firm, strict guidelines for the pack to obey. You dog is at her happiest when obeying and serving you. Whenever you *don't* provide very exacting, precise rules and directions your guy is going to become confused and frustrated.

She expects that you will be demanding of her. Thousands of years of survival have ingrained within the conscientiousness of the canine brain that endurance is predicated solely on a well defined pecking order and hierarchy.

The dog has endured for dozens of centuries because, *and only because*, somewhere buried in the most primeval recesses of their prehistoric brain lies their key to survival. The dog knows only one means of survival and that is strictly *actional togetherness* based on the four "C"s of the pack's ability to endure. They are: collaboration, cooperation, communication, and coordination. Also, by the way, the makings of a great herd dog.

Consequently, if *you* are not the leader of the pack: the actual *Alpha Dog*; then get ready for an extremely difficult, frustrating and eventually failing future with your dog.

If your dog should nip you, or any member of the family. If she refuses a collar or a lead. If she refuses to come when called. If she hesitates to obey any of your commands: then there you have it.

If any of the above apply; then you are definitely not the Alpha Dog deserving of her respect. And further, guess what? *She is proposing her candidacy for the position in your family.* She is presenting her resume` as Alpha to the others in the pack (family). Each time she rebuffs your wishes or commands, it is a clear demonstration of her repudiation of your authority. So...how do you like those dog biscuits?

You have to get "Alpha" with your dog. Alpha is an attitude—a posture. What are its components? Quiet confidence, dignity, and authority.

Or, if you are familiar with the theater: Stage presents which means stand tall, and demand attention.

Once you understand and are able to play the Alpha role, your dog will recognize you immediately. That's exactly how her mother acted. And further, there was never any question in her mind who was the boss when mother was around. In the litter, mom was always Alpha; no if's, and's, but's nor exceptions.

Just to digress here for a moment, the definition of "quiet confidence" means exactly that. Mom doesn't shout (bark) at her pups. She is much more subtle with her reprimands. Rather than shout, use a firm voice and a steady eye to project your meaning that you are in charge. Your dog will love you for it.

Yes, without a moment's hesitation, your dog will love you for it. No dog wants to be Alpha. It just means too much responsibility. Only in the absence of firm direction will a dog aspire to the Alpha status.

Remember the primordial brain is telling this pup that survival is based solely on the absolute leadership of the pack. And further, if you won't provide it, someone has to.

It is the compassionate autocrat who wills the continuance of the pack. Which means that only the willing subordinates guarantee peace, health and prosperity for the blissful contentment of all.

If you doubt this supposition, then ask yourself who your dog loves most in your family? It is certain to be the person, who trains and commands her obedience. Not necessarily the person, who just feeds, pets and demonstrates love for her; but rather, the person who dominates her.

For those of you who plan to use your English Shepherd in herding trials there is a reason behind her ability to roundup and control herd animals. In her mind, she is still a member of the wolf pack, except that in this pack, no one except the Alpha is allowed the kill. (Those who nip or rough-up the kill will be punished by Alpha).

All others in the pack are subordinate communal hunters to the Alpha and they had better follow direction immediately and exactly or else. No individual rewards will come except as offered by the leader. So the object is to assist the leader in surround and driving the "kill" (cow, sheep, goat, etc.) toward the Alpha for a successful hunt. Only Alpha decides the outcome of the hunt.

How do you establish or re-establish Alpha with your dog? Well, if you have ever had the opportunity to observe a wolf pack—and there is no denying that your dog is a direct descendant of the wolf–you will understand there are two absolutes involved.

First, obedience and second a total shunning if the first is ignored or refused.

Remember; always stand tall when dealing with your guy. Alpha is both an attitude and a posture. You suppose attitude with a quiet, stern voice and a steady eye. "Sit" is going to become your advantage over this guy.

Before he eats, goes out, plays, or get petted, he must "sit" first. If he refuses to "sit" then he does not eat. If he refuses to "sit" he does not get petted. Praise him when he does, shun him when he doesn't.

And, despite your guilt trip, if he refuses you, he absolutely does not eat. This method of dealing with your dog is a categorical imperative unless you want an out of control, less than domestic, wolf in your household.

Your English Shepherd is a nice guy. He is a nice guy because for hundreds of years before him nice guys like him were being nurture by caring, devoted shepherds, crofters and simple farmers.

Your guy is a direct descendant of those who grew to love, cherish and obey their masters and mistress' with an undying devotion that has defied definition beyond words. There are no definitions for his love, just as there are no limits for his love for you.

You're a lucky guy. My experience with these Shepherds as always, since my youth, has given me to believe that they will love you regardless of your fortunes or misfortunes. No matter how many times you appear before them, each of your entrances will be grand.

They will be thrilled to see you, and overjoyed with your company. Their spirits will soar as they display their happiness beyond measure just to have you near.

No measure of your neglect, your nonchalance, your indifference, your insouciance will deter or dissuade his love for you. I would even go so far as to guarantee that until such time as you own an English Shepherd, you have never truly experience true love, true devotion, and true dedication. And, you can take that to your significant other with full confidence.

And, that's the kind of guy your shepherd is.

Breeding Your Shepherd

Without going into a whole lot of specifics, I would like tell you about some of my experiences and adventures in breeding the English Shepherd.

If you are serious about breeding your dog, I have offered a couple of good references later in the appendix that will go into a great deal more detail for you.

But for now, just a couple of thoughts about what to expect when and if you decide to breed your dog.

First off, it is quite a simple experience. Actually your bitch does all the hard stuff. All you have to do is worry a lot. And, for the most part all your worries and anxieties will be for naught.

To begin with, when to breed your bitch is a no-brainer. She will come into heat sometime between six months and one year of age. It is rarely advisable to breed your girl during her first season. She is more than likely a little too young and immature to handle the responsibility of motherhood at this age. Most vets will agree that you should wait until at least her second season before breeding.

Dog's cycles, despite what you may read, actually are very erratic. They are very difficult to predict with any accuracy. A good guess will be they will come into heat about every six months, however, some may cycle as early as four months and some only once a year.

The heat cycle will last approximately three weeks on average, but again some may only last from seven to ten days.

You will first notice bleeding from the vulva, some swelling and possibly increased urination. Your female may even attempt to mount another dog if one is available. This is called the proestrus period and the female *will not allow* males to mate with her.

Normally, somewhere within eight and twelve days later she will enter the second phase of her season which is called estrus in which she will allow a male to service her. This part of her season will last from four to twenty-one days. Keep in mind that she does not discriminate and will breed with any male during this period.

Finally, she will go out of heat (diestrus) and she will be less willing to mate. This stage will last from seven to fourteen days.

Again, all of these durations are mostly rough estimates. Ideally you should have a male stud about during the bitches' entire season. I keep two unrelated males and really don't have to worry about when to breed. I simply let the stud run with the bitch as soon as I detect any bleeding, swelling or discharge of the vulva. She handles it from there and knows when to allow the stud to cover her.

I cautiously, during this time, make sure to keep the studs separated. Two males together with a bitch will absolutely guarantee a fight. You should also bear in mind that a bitch can be impregnated by more than one stud. Meaning within a single litter there could be more than one father.

A word should be mentioned about the stud. My experience has always been to observe a change in the temperament of the male as soon as I start using him for breeding purposes.

My big old pussy-cat male puppy, once introduced to mating, soon thereafter becomes a macho, posturing, testosterone motivated male. I don't mean to infer that he will become vicious; however, I would caution you that he is no longer the gentle old soul he was before being introduced to girl friends. He will become much more protective and possessive.

Once the breeding has taken place, there will be a "tie" between the two mating dogs. In effect, the male's penis is tied within the female's vagina until the exchange of seaman has taken place. This tie will last anywhere from a few minutes to a half hour. In many cases, the two will become facing in opposite directions. Tail to tail so to speak until separation occurs.

I always leave the two together until diestrus. They will continue to "tie" on successive days until her season ends.

Now, the rest is pretty much up to momma. The most important aspect of your responsibility to her is to insure that she gets plenty of exercise during her pregnancy.

I attribute lots of exercise to the fact that I have never had a bitch with difficult labor. Along with restricting her food intake, to insure that she doesn't get too fat, I believe that plenty of activity is the key to a healthy whelping period.

❧

Caring For Her Puppies

Let's get right to the point. Leave her alone! It has been my experience that anytime I interfere with a mom's birthing a lot of things do tend to go wrong.

Once, when I suspected one of my bitches was due, I insisted on keeping her inside the house with me in a quiet back room with a nice whelping box all snug and comfortable for her.

She continued to whine and carry-on until I let her out on a snowy, freezing day. Once outside, she immediately commenced to drop puppies around the yard in the snow. Of course, I was unnerved by her actions and called her back to the house. I then proceeded to retrieve pups from the snow.

By the time I got back to dealing with her, she was all comfy cozy licking her litter clean all snuggled on my bed. I lost three of her pups which taught me to never again interfere with mom and her choices of where she would like to deposit her litter.

Years later, I had a bitch due who was ensconced in a nice yard with a choice of three different dog houses to harbor her upcoming litter. She chose to whelp under a large spruce tree exposed to the elements.

Having previously learned a lesson about deciding on a birthing site for a bitch, I left her and her pups under the Spruce for a few days until a storm hit. Then I moved her litter into one of the dog houses. She was now content to raise her brood in a sensible dog house.

So let me define for you, your role in the birthing of your dam. *You are an observer.* Unless, you observe a lengthy labor that extends longer than six to eight hours, *leave her alone.* In fact; if all is going well which means a pup is popping out every ten to thirty minutes, then get out of the room with mom entirely.

She doesn't need you around, and indeed, you actually represent only a major distraction to the event.

As a matter of design, I don't handle the pups for three or four days after their birth. I realize that you are curious about them, but mom's concern for their wellbeing far outweighs your curiosity. Certainly, you must check to see if they are all living, but that should be the extent of your fussing with her pups.

There is always the chance that if you disturb mom too much, she will become confused with all the unnecessary activity and lay down on one or more of the pups resulting in suffocation.

In short, mother knows best. Leave her alone.

Another concern you should ignore is mom's appetite for a few days after the litter arrives. I once panicked and drove mom to the vet because she wasn't eating after giving birth. I was concerned that she would have to make lots of high protein milk for her pups and she should be eating.

The trip was a false alarm. It turned out to be about eighty dollars worth of false alarm to my wallet. She was fine. As distasteful as it may seem, for the first couple of weeks mom gets some of her necessary nourishment from cleaning up after the pups in the nest.

She actually drinks the puppies' urine and eats their feces. Oh! Gross me out, you say.

Think about it. Fifteen thousand years ago instinct told mother dogs that if predators could sniff out newborns, their waste or even their afterbirth, it would make for a very delicious meal for them. Therefore, instinct also told mom to get rid of any odors that might lead hungry carnivores to her den.

Also warmth is a primary consideration for puppies at this age. Newborn pups have very little ability to self-generate body heat. They depend solely upon mom for not only sustenance, but warmth. Another reason why mom can't be off hunting for her supper and leaving her pups to chill.

Not only does mom clean up in, and around her nest, she also indulges herself in a great deal of licking away any scent emanating from her young's genitals or anuses.

Today, none of my bitches whelp in the outdoor kennel. I now realize that because mom is so fastidious about cleaning up after her kids, it is much easier to have all her maternal activities take place in my study. There I can keep track of things. No fuss and no bother. And, I can get a good night's sleep without having to go outside to the kennel to check on things.

When the pups become three to four weeks old, they are moved outside to their new residents. At this age their eyes begin to open and they are able to navigate outside the nest. It is also about the time that clean-up becomes a bit too much for Mom. Because I don't want to share the housekeeping chores with her, I move the pups out to the kennel.

Now is the time to indulge your curiosity with the pups. You have a certain obligation to begin socializing the pups now, and introduce them to new environments and adventures.

It is now appropriate to handle them a great deal. Give them confidence in humans by turning them on their backs and cradling them. This is a very vulnerable position for pups and it lets them be assured that they have nothing to fear from you in this position.

Tickle all four of their feet to help them identify their senses. Give them the opportunity to walk on a number of different surfaces such as grass, tile, concrete, etc.

This is a good time to take the opportunity to check for tummy hernias. While you are cradling them on their backs, examine their bellies for protrusions that might indicate an abdominal hernia. It happens quite frequently with puppies and involves a localized hole, or defect through which adipose tissue or abdominal organs covered with peritoneum may protrude.

It involves a fairly simple surgical procedure to correct, and in many cases can be taken care of when the pup is either to be spayed or neutered.

At about six weeks of age it is time for a vet's visit for all the puppies. They should have a physical examination, all necessary temporary vaccines, and worm medication.

This would also be a good time to ask your vet for a signed "Health Certificate" for each of the pups. It will later represent a certificate of confidence you can present to the puppy's new owner. I expedite this procedure by providing the vet with blank copies of a health certificate that I make up on my home computer.

After the vet check, you are pretty much home free with the litter except for now finding them a good home.

Selling Your Pups

Your first obligation in finding a "good home" for each of your puppies is firstly an obligation to the puppy, and secondly to yourself.

You will sleep better at night if you spend more time culling out those unfit for puppy parenthood.

For those of you who cut corners when "culling", because you dread the thought of puppy leftovers, here's a thought: You are not doing a proper job of advertising and promoting your product if your pups are not flying out the kennel door...so to speak...when the time comes to find new homes for them.

Otherwise, you could be completely discerning and very selective when choosing new parents for your pups.

One of the first means of insuring the pup is going to a good home is to quote a price in keeping with the real value of the dog. Economical pets are throw-away pets and will be treated in kind.

Apart from that, all else is strictly gut feelings. You are either a good judge of character or you are not.

Forget requiring a signed contract. That's of little help and a complete copout when it comes to doing a proper job of discriminating among prospects.

I have a law degree and I can tell you without fear of contradiction that mandating a signed agreement to faithfully love, honor and care for the new puppy is one-hundred percent unenforceable.

Usually courts will rely on the judgment of Animal Control Officers to decide whether a change of venue is necessary for an animal, and whether or not proceedings are justified.

Which reminds me of when I lived in Manhattan, and when landlords would take tenets to court for violating their lease agreements by keeping dogs in their apartment?

Never in the history of Big Apple jurisprudence would a judge, who had to face reelection, ever evict someone's pet from a domicile.

Neither would a judge arbitrarily adjudicate puppy custody if she cared to get reelected.

So it is up to you to read the character carefully of your prospective buyers. One clue to responsible puppy ownership would be to ask if the buyer currently has, or has recently owned a dog. Ask if he has children at home. Contrary to what J.C. Fields once said: "A person who *loves* kids and dogs can't be all bad".

One of the most reliable means of judging the buyer is to require multiple conversations about the puppy in question. Listen very carefully regarding their motive(s) for purchasing the pup.

I mentioned earlier the term: "puppy leftovers". I mean having puppies that are three months old and still unsold with no prospects of a new home. This situation can only mean that you probably can use some help with "English Shepherd Marketing 101".

First off, you need a website. A website doesn't mean you have to seek sales all across the country. You don't have to rely on shipping pups either because shipping is costly and time consuming. That long drive to the airport is not only time consuming, but tedious.

Your drive to the airport also adds somewhere between $250 and $350 to the cost of the pup. Actually with the proper marketing and promotion, all of your pups can easily be sold locally.

Not that occasionally shipping puppy is a bad thing. I have bought pups from other States and had them shipped in because I wanted to acquire fresh bloodlines for my pedigrees of the future.

I have also been approached by prospects who needed my kennel bloodlines and I willing shipped pups to them.

My "movie pups"; Trixie and Dixie, who now belong to Canine Costars, were both shipped across the country so they could take advantage of a great opportunity in show business.

However, it goes without saying that if you are spending a lot of time and resources shipping puppies, there could be a better way.

There is a rule of thumb among breeders that says you should spend the equivalent of the price of one puppy to promote and consummate the sale of the entire litter.

That seems a little high in my estimation; however, whoever those powers may be, they are on the right track.

A friend once came to Howard Hughes to borrow $10,000 to establish an airline that would carry US Mail. Howard insisted such a sum could only mean the airline would be undercapitalized and consequently fail. He gave the friend $100,000 instead. That airline became TWA.

It's the old saw that says: you have to spend a buck to make a buck. But, it also implies you spend that buck wisely.

Therefore; following is that quick course in English Shepherd Marketing 101.

The website is the key. Creating a website for the sale of your dogs and puppies should not be a scary thing. Today there are a number of good site providers with excellent and easy editing tools to use.

I have used Homestead.com[36] for years and they have made lots of money for me selling my goat kids, bunnies, and puppies. With Homestead it's so easy even a caveman can do it.

I get so frustrated surfing through websites that don't understand the first principals of marketing. These principals quite simply are: Who are you, what are you, where are you and why are you.

Just like journalism's five "W's", except for the "when", you have to get all of that up front and in the lead part of your story. For the most part buyers are impatient and will not spend a lot of time investigating how they can purchase a puppy from your confusing website.

In fact, always get the main idea right up front in big, bold letters: PUPPIES AVAILABLE FOR SALE.

Now that Internet Surfer knows you have puppies for sale, what do they look like? Folks love to shop catalogs, especially Internet surfers. So make your site a puppy catalog. Take lots of time to add really cute pictures of the available puppies. A picture is worth a thousand words.

Go to the mall and buy some plastic flowers, cheap toys, and gadgets for background in your puppy photos to add novelty to your photo shoot. And, remember to get in close with the camera. Good photography looks closely at the subject. *We don't care to see the rest of your living room, or your front yard...just the puppy please.*

Now, you are beginning to ask why all of this emphasis on the Internet if you are not going to ship puppies? Simply because why should you ship puppies with all that additional cost and bother when you can, with an effective local advertising campaign and a good puppy catalog on the internet, sell your entire brood locally?

Here's the solution to an effective sales campaign. A classified ad in the local newspaper is not capable of *telling your whole story.* The story of how you have the most beautiful puppies in all of doggydom for sale. Puppies that are so unique in their appeal they will require an entire book, or multiple web pages to describe.

Here's an important rub. You are selling a "country dog" so don't waste your advertising dollars on a lot of city slickers.

In fact, my advertising surveys repeatedly have offered the conclusion that if you are going to sell locally; your ad should appeal to country folk. That doesn't necessarily preclude the city prospects, because they too read country publications.

So rather than invest your advertising dollars in big city newspaper classifieds–much too expensive–look around for the country type weeklies and "Want Ad Digests". In fact today, after wasting lots of advertising dollars on big city papers, I now advertise exclusively in rural/suburban type publications.

You might well take exception to my classifying the English Shepherd exclusively as a "Country Dog". Well, my reasoning here is predicated on another rule of Marketing.

Quaintly put: *"You sell what the other feller aint got to sell."*

You're English Shepherds are never going to compete with the Schnauzer, the Shih Tzu or the Shiba Inu in the pet category, so give it up. Make the most of what you have got. And, my sales recorders indicate us English Shepherd breeders have got a lot to capitalize on.

To begin with the first line in my classified ad always *and without exception reads*: "Old Fashion Farm Collie puppies for sale". The second line reads: "Registered English Shepherds".

I have found this approach to be appealing to buyers who are looking for not only something different, but are also looking for something nostalgic. Heck, most puppy buyers don't know what an English Shepherd is anyway, so why feature the breed name in the first line of your classified?

So many of my buyers have confided that their dad used to talk about these dogs, or they have heard about this breed, but didn't think it existed any longer. Some relate old family histories about their farm dogs and the many myths, tales and legends about the "old fashion farm collie". That's something Shih Tzu breeders haven't got to offer. So make the most of it.

The second feature I like to emphasis in my classified ads is the phrase: "love kids". You cannot imagine how appealing this is to parents of small children. Again, in my surveys, this simple phrase is often cited as indicative of why the prospective buyer became curious about the breed and wanted to explore more information about the English Shepherd.

I am fortunate because I live in a rural area that has several country presses available to accept my classifieds.

There is a Wantad Digest that offers a slick magazine type publication. A two-week posting costs only $29.95 and will feature four of your photos, your copy, an Email address, a URI (Uniform Resource Identifier) to your website, your telephone number, and your general home area location. This same advertisement is also available simultaneously on the internet for web surfers to notice. That's the bargain advertising media that sells dozens of puppies for me.

I am fortunate to also have a couple of those "freebie" advertising country tabloids that are sometimes mailed and sometimes just stacked in malls for the taking. The advertising rates are usually so reasonable that you almost can't afford not to sponsor a classified in one of their publications.

Again, I favor the "country" type papers because it is so difficult to compete in the big city dailies alongside the multi-colored Labs, Retrievers, and the ever popular Bichon Frise, the Rottweiler, the Labradoodle, and the Lhasa Apso dogs.

You would also be wise, if you own a computer, to make up a color poster with pictures of your dogs and puppies to post in feed stores, farm stores, and pet supply shops.

And, speaking of computers it is easy, economical, and practical to make up some business cards listing your dog breed and other contact information for just pennies. Business cards are good for 'year round advertising. You can buy specialty business card blanks or just 24 pound 8 by 11 paper stock at the local mall. More than likely you already have the software installed on your computer to create business cards.

Here is the last best shot at successful English Shepherd marketing. You have enticed the customer to your kennel and closed the sale.

Now for the customer satisfaction follow-up that will help spread the word unto the entire doggy world that you are an honest person of integrity and a responsible breeder of the finest pet known to man. Yes, you must pay strict attention to the all important word of mouth marketing asset. Your reputation must precede you.

Therefore, take the time and make the effort to create an owners "puppy packet" to present to each buyer when they come to pickup puppy.

Again, if you own a computer or have a friend with a computer, this is a must if you want to encourage future sales of your English Shepherd puppies.

What should the packet include?

How about a receipt of sale, a health certificate signed by your vet and including a record of current vaccines she has given the pup.

Also, you could include an information statement guaranteeing that this puppy is free of any known disease or illness and has no known congenital hereditary conditions that might adversely affect the health of the animal at the time of sale.

Further, you should include: A copy of the sire and dam's pedigree, a United Kennel Club blank registration form (download from the web), a statement accounting for the benefits of spaying and neutering, a Rabies information sheet, and a statement regarding consumer rights pertaining to pet sales in your home State.

Some States have a program to license kennels. Although I don't quality as a wholesale/retail pet dealer, New York State offers a voluntary program for smaller pet breeders to obtain certification.

On both a routine and random schedule, a representative from the Department of Agriculture and Markets will inspect my dogs, their kennel along with my sales and breeding records to insure conformation to sound principals of kennel operations.

Such inspections help to insure that all the animals are treated properly. They must have the necessary licenses, vaccines, and medications as well as be properly groomed and fed. Breeding records will reveal any abuse of multiple litters from individual dams. New York State is a leader in discouraging puppy mills.

I believe being a licensed breeder[37] helps to instill confidence for the discerning puppy buyer.

Does this seem like a lot of work for you? Not as much work as keeping a couple of leftover aging puppies about the place. Not half the anxiety of wondering whether or not you will be able to finally sell them.

Follow these simple suggestions and you can eliminate both the headache and the heart ache the difficult task of finding suitable homes for your puppies entail.

Your Moral and Legal Obligations

Of course, you have a moral obligation to provide and care for your English Shepherd with prudence and forethought.

But, many dog owners are unaware of their legal obligations, as well as the legal ramifications of pet ownership. First off, there are not only the license requirements set by most municipalities, but many States, cities, towns and counties also have other mandated requirements, conditions, prerequisites, and constraints to be fulfilled as a privilege of dog ownership.

Here is one of the most asked legal questions pertaining to pet ownership–and quickly; *no*, upon your passing, you can't leave the family homestead, jewels or fortune to your English Shepherd.

One of the most misunderstood aspects of dog ownership is first its legal definition. Your dog is not a legal entity. He is your property, and as such you cannot leave your estate to him anymore than you can leave your estate to your favorite reclining lounge chair.

If you do name him as your beneficiary any such bequeaths will instead go to your alternate or residual beneficiary.

There are several alternatives to providing for your dog(s) after your death. The most obvious is, of course, to choose a new owner. Very simply in your will: "I leave my dog Shep in the loving care of my brother Tom."

Don't surprise your brother either. Make sure that he is aware well in advance of his forthcoming inheritance. And further, Shep is going to be a whole lot more welcome at Tom's place if he arrives with a token of his gratitude. A few bucks for some dog bones and vet fees might make his welcome more inviting.

Again a simple covenant stating: "Should I predecease my dog Shep, I leave $5,000 to be used for his care to my Brother Tom. If Tom is unable to care for him, then the $5,000 fund along with Shep shall go to my Sister Mary for his care".

You should be aware, however, that although the part about leaving Tom the $5,000 is both legal and enforceable, the part about your brother using the money for the care and upkeep of Shep is questionable. He might very well use the money to run off with your widow. And, there would be no recourse.

On the other hand, should Shep predecease you, Tom won't get the money. The money, along with any other property that the will doesn't specifically give away, will go in with your residual unspecified funds and to the person named to receive your miscellany.

If, however, you still insist on leaving some of your property to Shep there are currently about 30 States who will consider a trust for your dog. This is just another means of putting someone else in charge of caring for Shep after your death. In most cases you will name a trustee who is charged with following your written set of instructions.

Another means of providing for your pet after your death is to make an arrangement for him to be humanely destroyed. Don't count on such a covenant being carried out. If your final wish for your dog to be destroyed is to be carried out by any surrogate it is hard to believe any judge would actually adjudicate putting a happy, healthy dog to sleep if an alternative is available.

Many States, about 20, today have a bill of rights for pet buyers. If you are either a buyer or a seller, and even if you are not governed by State regulations, you should be familiar with these laws.

Here is a primary list of questions every buyer should have answers for:
- Where did the dog come from?
- What is his health history?
- When and where was it born?
- What are his warranties?

Perhaps, if you are a seller, you should go back to the previous Chapter and look again at the "Puppy Packet" and the materials that I propose should be included. I doubt with such documentation of the sale a buyer would have any recourse against you.

Now, as a buyer, even if your State doesn't have specific laws regarding the sale of dogs and cats you may seek relief under what is called an "express warranty". Because, as we mentioned earlier, dogs are considered property their sale is subject to the same rules as used cars and lame horses.

That is to say that if the seller promises you something (expresses verbally) and you decide *based upon that promise* to purchase the dog; the law considers this expression by the seller a warranty. Should the puppy not live up to the sellers verbal promises than you have grounds to sue for your money back?

There is also available to you, but much harder to establish, an implied warranty. That is to say the seller didn't actually make a verbal promise, but did imply certain attributes or characteristics about the dog that did or did not later materialize. This becomes a question of "he said–I said" and very difficult to substantiate.

An implied warranty is very difficult to establish in court with two very real exceptions.

Merchantability is that implied promise in the sale that any reasonably *prudent* person should expect from any type of similar product. It doesn't matter that the seller didn't specifically promise the puppy didn't have an umbilical hernia. The buyer has an implied right to expect his puppy was healthy at the time of the sale. Again, the test of Implied Merchantability is: What would any reasonably, prudent buyer expect?

Fitness of purpose is another implied warranty that is almost always enforceable. If, for instance, you are looking for a herding dog for your farm and the seller knows this and recommends a dog named "City Dude". You later discover that City Dude is deathly afraid of sheep, cows, goats and baby chicks along with anything country, your seller has obviously breached the implied warranty of *fitness* and you do have recourse for a refund.

Further there may be an implied warranty when the seller puts too much emphasis on the fact that both parents of the pup have been OFA' ed or PennHip'ed. Be careful not to imply that the offspring, because of their parents excellent x-ray results, will be equally free of osteoarthritis disease. Using today's technology, a puppy can be PennHip'ed as young as 16 weeks, and should the results not equal that of the parent's, the seller may be subject to litigation stemming from an implied warranty.

If you are unhappy or dissatisfied with your puppy after you get him home, promptly–usually within 30 days–tell the seller in writing. If you have a written agreement you should refer to it. Keep a copy of your letter. You can also mail a copy to yourself and leave the envelope sealed to establish the postmarked date of your original complaint.

If your seller doesn't satisfactorily respond, then you must consider small claims court.

Of course there are myriad and diverse laws on the books pertaining to pet ownership, and it is because of their numbers and diversity that it would be impossible to detail even a limited number of these laws and ordinances. State laws vary considerably and whatever a pet owner may be accountable for in one jurisdiction may not hold true in another.

Safe to say, in most instances, common sense will hold sway.

English Shepherd's really enjoy having company visit.

Afterword

If you currently own an English Shepherd, or you are thinking of buying a pup this book is not intended be an end all and be all, but is intended as a good beginning for rising your puppy to become a fine upstanding canine citizen.

Apart from reading this book, there is a host of other resources on the Internet, as well as the many reference books about dog husbandry on Amzon.com.

I believe it is infinitely rewarding to join one of the English Shepherd clubs or associations so that you may be able to keep up with the latest developments with the breed, as well as use their discussion groups on the web as a good resource for helping to both train and enjoy your English Shepherd.

One of my most favorite stories about the loyalty and devotion of the English Shepherd harks back to a book about "Old Shep". This is the story of the bond between a sheep dog and his shepherd. Near Fort Benton, Montana, when an old sheepherder passed away, his coffin was shipped back east.

Shep watched his master's coffin being loaded onto a train and from that day forward, this loyal dog met every passenger train that arrived at the Fort Benton Depot for the next five years with hopes that he would again see the old man who had cared for him. Through snow and rain and cold he slept under the depot platform, and once the station manager and townspeople notice him and discovered the details of his life, they adopted him and cared for this loyal shepherd for the remainder of his life.

There is a monument built in his honor in Fort Benton. Still today, people visit the grave of a dog whose actions remind us of the true meaning of loyalty, love, and devotion. There is a children's book titled: Shep: Our Most Loyal Dog by Sneed B. Collard III which also has some excellent illustrations.

I can recall a time one snowy cold morning while living in a cabin up on the Great Sacandaga Lake, when I decided I needed to shop for some milk and butter. On my way out to the truck, I whistled for Shep, but he was nowhere about so I drove on off to a farm about twelve miles away on the old Military Road. At this farm some nice folks sold maple syrup, raw milk, home baked bread, and home churned butter.

I soon returned to the cabin and immediately stoked up the fire for the wind began to blow and the storm was rapidly becoming a blizzard. After a bit, I began to become concerned about Shep. I went outside a couple of times to whistle for him, but the winds by then were howling pretty good. I decided he couldn't hear me calling. It was nightfall when there was a pounding on the cabin door. Outside on the stoop stood one of the town workers wrapped in several layers of inclement weather gear. He immediately inquired if I was missing my dog. When I assured him that I was indeed missing Shep; he said he had been plowing highways all day and had seen my collie several times traversing the Old Military Road. He offered me a ride in the town plow and we headed for the Military Road. Sure enough, as we approached the old farm house where I had shopped that morning, there was Shep pacing forth and back on the porch happy as a lost child to be discovered. What a relief for the both of us to be reunited.

I can only surmise, that the morning, when I left the cabin I whistle for Shep, but in my impatience to get started, I didn't wait long enough for him to arrive at the truck. He must have followed the scent way up to the Military Road; but then as the snow deepened he more than likely lost the scent to find his way home. Unlike a lot of folks who get lost in a snowstorm, that good old dog knew enough to go back (where for him my scent was strongest) and wait for me to find him. I think the lesson of this story for me was that Shep was such a friendly good old dog, more of the townspeople knew him better than they knew me.

Then there was Jenny, an English Shepherd I bought when I lived in Georgia. Although I had a nice townhouse in Atlanta, being a born and bred Yankee country boy, I decided it would be nice to own a little weekend farm up in Cherokee County, Ga. This was one of those rural counties that boasted they were the Broiler Capital of the World; and as such, my next door neighbor down the road housed 65,000 broilers on his place.

It seems that when ready for market, large trailer trucks would back into the facility and load these thousands of chickens for transport.

Apparently, it was the morning after one of these frenzied chicken catching session next door that Jenny was missing. After my morning coffee, I strolled out into the backyard and whistled for her, but she didn't appear. I thought this a bit odd, because Jenny was always a very obedient girl. After whistling and calling to no avail, I decided to walk down to the branch (Southern lingo for creek) on the backend of the property.

There, sure enough, I found Jenny. Happy and proud as can be, because during the night fifteen or twenty broilers must have escaped my neighbors nocturnal melee...and as far as Jenny was concerned they were not going to remain fugitives as long as she was on duty. She had those broilers rounded up and secure. Of course, although I was whistling and calling for her, she hesitated to leave her duty post and allow these runaways their freedom.

What a good laugh my neighbor and I had over Jenny, the chicken herding dog. He said he had never heard of such a thing and offered to buy Jenny many times over.

Some years later, when I returned north and was living on a small homestead in Upstate New York, Jenny once again came to the rescue. I woke one morning to discover dairy cows grazing my lawn and my fields across the road from my house. It was a large herd of at least forty or fifty big Holstein cows.

I got dressed and along with Jenny managed to roundup the nearby bovines into a smaller cluster, and then I sent Jenny down into the nearby wood to rustle out the strays to join the main herd. We had the situation well under control when the owner of the deserters arrives by pickup with a gang of teenage boys on the back.

I said: "Do you want my dog to take them home?"

He said: "No, my boys will drive them back."

Well, you never saw such a rodeo in your life as six or seven teenage boys trying to herd that many cows back down the road to their home. It was a hullabaloo beyond description. The return of the bovines was a ruckus that went on for hours. Those boys must have been exhausted by day's end; however, had those modern—day dairy farmers been at all familiar with cow dogs, they would have understood that Jenny could have had those miscreant bossies home posthaste sans hassle. As Jenny and I sat on the front porch that morning watching this teenage/bos stampede, I think I caught just a glint of derisive snicker in her eye movements that morning, and I also think I heard a slight chortle of contempt in her throat.

Following is my last English Shepherd story...I promise...but like an old comedian, Jimmy Durante, use to quip: "I got a million of 'em".

Bunkie, a beautiful tri-color, was without a doubt my most sensitive English Shepherd. I often referred to her as my canine chiropractor. Now I have read many accounts of dogs that were able to detect various maladies, and in fact recently have read of dogs being trained to sniff out cancer in patients.

But, it took me a while to understand the antics of Bunkie. Here was a time when I was suffering chronic severe lower back pain, and would often wake in the morning with soreness and discomfort. Bunkie, as was her habit, routinely slept on the floor of my bedroom. But, as my symptoms escalated, more and more she was inclined to jump up on the bed with me in the early mornings. Eventually, it became her practice to snuggle her back close against my lower spine, brace her feet securely into the mattress, and apply pressure to my afflicted aching back. And then once again, brace her feet to better her grip, and once more apply pressure to my torment.

The result was phenomenal and verging on the unbelievable. As the morning canine chiropractic treatments continued, there seem to be a gradual lessening of my discomfort altogether.

Of course, it goes without saying that my relief could well have been the result of other therapy factors, or medication...or the eventual termination of my pain could be ascribed to predictable remission.

But, needless to say, deep within the recesses of my psyche, I attribute my spinal remedy to the miraculous restorative powers of Bunkie. And, I seriously doubt any HMO is going to take exception to that theory.

Well enough. I am certain you will forgive a cranky old man his jabbering and his boasting when it comes to relating tales about his love for his dogs. I can only hope that, one day in your old age; you might be both blessed and enriched with an abundance of happy memories and a profusion of tales relating countless moments of love and merriment associated with your faithful Farm Collie.

"Bye for now, come see us again."

End Notes

[1] http://www.englishshepherdsunited.org

[2] http://www.englishshepherd.org/club

[3] http:/www.farmcollie.com/

[4] http://www.nesr.info

[5] www.UKCdogs.com

[6] http://englishshepherdsunited.org

[7] http://www.englishshepherd.org/club

[8] The Culture Clash by Jean Donaldson.

[9] Mother knows Best, The Natural Way to Train Your Dog, by Carol Lea Benjamin.

[10] Dog Talk, Training your dog through a canine point of view, by John Ross and Barbara McKinney

[11] The Culture Clash by Jean Donaldson

[12] Don't Shoot the Dog by Karen Pryor

[13] The Beginner's Guild to Agility by Laurie Leach

[14] http://www.affordableagility.com/

[15] http://www.englishshepherdsunited.org/index.html

[16] http://www.farmcollie.com/

[17] http://www.stockdog.com/index.html

[18] http://www.e-trainingfordogs.com/HerdingMaster.html

[19] http://www.k9station.com/stockdog.htm?#N

[20] http://www.northeastherdinginfo.com/trainers.htm

[21] http://www.flyball.org/

[22] http://www.flyballdogs.com/locator.html#new_york

[23] http://www.apdt.com/

[24] http://www.asca.org/

[25] http://www.englishshepherdsunited.org/page13.html[28]

[26] http://www.worldcaninefreestyle.org/intro_history.htm

[27] http://www.musicaldogsport.org/index.htm

[28] http://www.canine-freestyle.org/

[29] http://www.golden-dogs.org/

[30] www.petdiets.com

[31] http://www.barfworld.com/

[32] http://www.vegetariandogs.com/

[33] "Real Food for Dogs" by Arden Moore

[34] Gourmet Dog Biscuits from Your Bread Machine by Sondra Macdonald

[35] Three Dog Bakery by Dan Dye and Mark Beckloff

[36] http://www.hammondenglishshepherds.com

[37] New York State Pet Dealer's license #PD 00537

Appendix

Some references for your continued study in becoming a knowledgeable dog owner

"Don't Shoot the Dog, The New Art of Teaching and training"	By Karen Pryor
"Mother Knows Best, The Natural Way to Train Your Dog"	By Carol Lea Benjamin
"How to Speak Dog, Mastering the Art of Dog–Human Communication"	By Stanley Coren
"On Talking Terms With Dogs: Calming Signals"	By Turid Rugaas
"Dog Talk, Training your Dog through a Canine Point of View"	By John Ross, Barbara McKinney
"The Culture Clash"	By Jean Donaldson
"The Complete Book of Dog Breeding"	By Dan Rice, D.V.M.
"Book of the Bitch"	By J.M. Evans & Kay White
"Every Dog's Legal Guide"	By Mary Randolph, J.D.
"Real Food for Dogs, 50 Vet Approved Recipes"	By Arden Moore
"Gourmet Dog Biscuits, From your Bread Machine"	By Sondra Macdonald
"Three Dog Bakery Cookbook"	By Dan Dye & Mark Beckloff
"First Aid for Dogs: What to do When Emergencies Happen"	By Bruce Fogle
"Dog Owner's Veterinary Handbook"	By James M. Giffin, M.D.

ॐ

English Shepherd Breed Clubs:

The United English Shepherd Association, Inc.
Connie DeBusschere, President
http://www.englishshepherdsunited.org/index.html

The English Shepherd Club
Mary Peaslee, President
http://www.englishshepherd.org/

American Working Farmcollie Association
Erin Hischke, Registrar
http://www.farmcollie.com/contact.htm

Made in the USA